To Swede
from
Harold Jr.

THE BATTLE OF
CAPE ESPERANCE

THE BATTLE OF CAPE ESPERANCE

ENCOUNTER AT GUADALCANAL

CAPTAIN CHARLES COOK, *USN (Ret.)*

NAVAL INSTITUTE PRESS
Annapolis, Maryland

Naval Institute Press edition, 1992, published by arrangement with HarperCollins Publishers.

Maps by Donald T. Pitcher

LIBRARY OF CONGRESS CATALOGING-IN-PUBLICATION DATA

Cook, Charles O. (Charles Olney), 1911–
    The Battle of Cape Esperance : encounter at Guadalcanal / Charles
Cook. — Naval Institute Press ed.
        p.   cm.
    Originally published: New York : Crowell, c1968.
    Includes bibliographical references and index.
    ISBN 1-55750-126-2
    1. Guadalcanal Island (Solomon Islands), Battle of, 1942–1943.
2. World War, 1939–1945—Campaigns—Solomon Islands—Esperance,
Cape.   3. Esperance, Cape (Solomon Islands)—History.   I. Title.
D767.98.C6   1992
940.54′26—dc20   92-4658

9 8 7 6 5 4 3 2

To REAR ADMIRAL GILBERT C. HOOVER, USN (RET.),
WITH THE RESPECT AND AFFECTION FELT
BY ALL WHO SERVED UNDER HIM IN THE LIGHT CRUISER *Helena*
DURING THOSE TOUGH DAYS IN THE SOUTH PACIFIC.

PREFACE

IT HAS BEEN DIFFICULT to write this account. The Battle of Cape Esperance was fought in the dark and no single witness saw very much of what took place. The earliest accounts, the action reports of the ships and other commands engaged in the battle, suffer from that trouble. They are my primary sources. Twenty-five years after the event I have tried, through interview and correspondence, to bridge gaps and reconcile differences. I have consulted such Japanese sources as I could locate. The result, I believe, is a more complete and accurate story than has heretofore existed, but one still susceptible of revision when new evidence turns up. Inevitably, the friends who kindly took trouble to answer my questions will find that their answers, or sometimes even the action reports submitted over their own signatures, have been disregarded in some particular. My only excuse is that, faced with conflicting evidence, I was forced to reject some of it in order to get on with the story. I used the best judgment I could but admit freely to the possibility of error. For such errors as I have committed, I humbly apologize.

The American forces at Guadalcanal were keeping Zone Minus Eleven time, the Japanese Zone Minus Nine. I have converted all times taken from the Japanese records to Zone Minus Eleven in the interest of clarity.

I consulted the following published material in preparing this account:

THE STRUGGLE FOR GUADALCANAL, Vol. V of *History of United States Naval Operations in World War II* by Samuel E. Morison.

THE PACIFIC—GUADALCANAL TO SAIPAN, Vol. IV of *The Army Air Forces in World War II,* W. F. Craven and J. L. Cate, eds.

STRATEGY AND COMMAND: THE FIRST TWO YEARS, by Louis Morton, in the series *The United States Army in World II.*

GUADALCANAL: THE FIRST OFFENSIVE, by John Miller, in the same series.

PEARL HARBOR TO GUADALCANAL, by Hough, Ludwig, and Shaw, Vol. I of *History of U. S. Marine Corps Operations in World War II.*

A HISTORY OF COMMUNICATIONS—ELECTRONICS IN THE UNITED STATES NAVY, by Captain L. S. Howeth, USN.

THE PROCEEDINGS of the United States Naval Institute for the letter of Lieutenant (jg) George T. Weems and the observations of Vice Admiral R. Tanaka appearing in the August 1962 and July 1956 issues, respectively.

I extend sincere thanks to:

Rear Admiral Ernest M. Eller, Ret., Director of Naval History, and Doctor M. Maurer, Department of the Air Force, for access to the official records pertaining to this battle and for the cheerful assistance given by them and others under their direction.

Mr. Susumi Nishiura, Chief, War History Office, Japanese Defense Agency, for access to official Japanese records; Mr. Yuzuru Sanematsu, for translating them; Mr. Roger Pineau of the Smithsonian Institution for directing me to them; and Mr. John R. Edwards, who translated other material.

Mr. William D. F. Morrisson, once an air intelligence officer at Henderson Field, for information concerning that spot. Commander Frank B. Correia, USN, Ret., for information concerning weapons and armor performance.

The Office of the Assistant Secretary of Defense for Public Affairs, the Office of Naval History, Marine Corps Headquarters, and the National Archives for making available the photographs used in this book.

I am particularly indebted to those listed below, all participants in the Battle of Cape Esperance or the events surrounding it, and most now retired, who have taken the time to search their memories and offer a quantity of information which is indispensable to an understanding of what happened:

Vice Admirals R. E. Wilson, E. B. Taylor, W. G. Cooper, and J. L. Chew; Rear Admirals G. C. Hoover, G. B. Carter, E. T. Seaward, R. D. Smith, T. H. Kobey, C. L. Carpenter, J. T. Brewer, W. W. Wilbourne, W. C. Butler, D. D. Hawkins, Bruce McCandless, L. J. Kirn, and E. A. Barham; Brigadier General L. G. Saunders, USAF; Captains A. G. Beckmann, F. B. T. Myhre, T. A. Brown, G. A. O'Connell, C. M. Lee, L. J. Baird, W. C. Boles, and A. H. Damon; Commanders M. T. Tyng and J. H. Lambert; Chief Warrant Officer A. J. Squires; and Chief Petty Officer C. W. Morgan.

Finally, I am deeply grateful to my wife who assisted in many ways, not least of which was the typing of the manuscript.

CONTENTS

ILLUSTRATIONS

PHOTOS
Following page 78

Army Air Force B-17

Curtis SOC

Northwest tip of Guadalcanal near Cape Esperance

Grumman F4F Wildcat of a U.S. Marine fighter squadron

MAPS

THE BATTLE OF
CAPE ESPERANCE

Chapter One

GUADALCANAL

AT SUNSET ON SUNDAY, October 11, 1942, a formation of U.S. warships steamed northwest near latitude 11 degrees south, longitude 160 degrees east. Four of the ships—cruisers *San Francisco, Boise, Salt Lake City,* and *Helena*—were in column. The others, destroyers *Farenholt, Duncan, Laffey, McCalla,* and *Buchanan,* fanned out ahead and on the bows of the column in an antisubmarine screen. Together the cruiser column with its destroyer screen maintained an arrow-shaped formation. Arrow and ships pointed in the same direction.

The ships made no smoke, but they squatted slightly, bows up and sterns down—a sure indicator of high speed. Their wakes trailed in narrow carpets of white foam which faded astern on the gentle surface of the sea. The horizon was empty except for a massive cumulus cloud towering to the east.

The formation's destination was the vicinity of Cape Esperance, 120 miles distant on the northwest corner of Guadalcanal. The Cape was the terminus for shipping supporting Japanese troops fighting U.S. Marines on that island. The nine U.S. warships comprised Task Group 64.2 of the South Pacific Force. They were speeding to intercept the enemy and break a stalemate, if possible, in a campaign without precedent.

Task Group Commander was Rear Admiral Norman Scott in *San Francisco.* He was present, commanding a group of support ships, when the Marines first landed at Guadalcanal. Twenty miles of water had separated Scott from the other support group which, at the Battle of Savo Island, was surprised in the dark, quickly overwhelmed, and destroyed by an enemy who departed as rapidly as he had hit.

Scott was too far off to help that night, but close enough to feel the

1

humiliation of defeat. Since that disaster, he had seen the situation in the South Pacific deteriorate even further. Now he was leading an attempt to reverse that trend—an effort that was hazardous, if only because it had to be made amid all the uncertainties of darkness.

Subordinates instinctively scrutinize their leader on the eve of battle; they look for a hint of what he thinks will come. Aboard the flagship *San Francisco* on this evening, the prevailing mood of confidence was due, in large part, to the unchanging demeanor of the Admiral. There was a sense, a feeling, that a decision had been made, that a period of doubt was about to be ended. Beyond the northwest horizon, drawing in the American ships like a magnet, lay Guadalcanal.

The two-month-old struggle for that island was unusual. The island itself was of little value. Roughly an oblong covering about twenty-five hundred square miles, it was a jungle and mountain wilderness with open stretches where grass grew taller than a man. The struggle taking place was concerned only incidentally with most of this inhospitable terrain. The prize—what really mattered—was an airfield. The field, scarcely a square mile of land, was the single objective for which every man was killed, every ship sunk, every plane shot down on both sides. The side that could firmly secure and use that airfield would gain an important advantage in the contest for supremacy in the South Pacific.

The Japanese had occupied Guadalcanal at the end of June, 1942, and immediately started to build the field. But in the first U.S. offensive ground action of the Pacific war American Marines landed a little more than a month later, drove the Japanese into the jungle, and held them off while completing the work the Japanese had started.

The American offense, however, soon became an exhausting defense. The Japanese struck back hard. It was a new type of operation. The field had to be seized, defended, and developed by men on the ground; it had to be shielded and supplied from the sea. Yet ultimately all of these efforts would fail unless planes from the field could defend it in the air. The ground, sea, and air forces of each side became so closely involved and dependent on one another that theoretical distinctions between "sea power," "air power," and other categories of military strength were blurred. U.S. naval ships hammered the artillery positions and supply dumps of enemy ground forces.

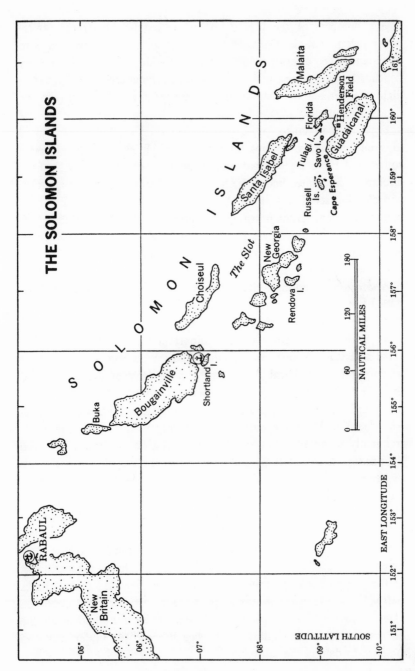

THE SOLOMON ISLANDS

3

Heavy bombers of the U.S. Army made regular long-range, over-water reconnaissance flights in the contest for the sea approaches to the island. U.S. aircraft, which sank enemy ships and strafed enemy beaches by day, were caught on the field by Japanese naval gunfire at night and threatened continuously by ground forces concealed in the dense, surrounding jungle.

Even in their customary roles, the separate services encountered unusual conditions. Troops moved in a jungle so thick that even a squad leader had difficulty at times keeping track of his men. At first, aircraft maintenance had to be handled in the open between air raids and cloudbursts. Pilots spent the night in foxholes and took off on combat missions in the morning with no rest and little breakfast. Offshore, there were nights when ships with guns that could throw a ton-and-a-half projectile fifteen miles were engaged at distances of less than one.

Appropriately enough, the intelligence apparatus that provided the Allied forces (air and naval units of Australia and New Zealand participated) with information was just as unusual as the battle conditions. Stationed secretly on every important island between Guadalcanal and Rabaul were one or more Coast Watchers, who had been organized by the Royal Australian Navy. Many of these men had lived in the islands for some years before the war. They knew the islands and the natives. They successfully enlisted native support even with the Japanese in occupation. Changing their observation posts frequently to avoid discovery, they observed and reported by radio the passage of enemy ships and aircraft and the arrival and departure of troops.

They rescued stranded seamen and airmen and arranged for their clandestine evacuation. Their reports were sometimes so good that air raids could be accurately predicted and prepared for at the Guadalcanal field an hour or more before the enemy planes arrived. The progress of bombers taking off at Rabaul, 550 miles to the northwest in the chain of islands, might be successively reported several times before the radar picked them up. As a result, the field could be cleared, fighters had ample time to climb to altitude and await the enemy, and ships unloading at the beach could get under way and prepare to defend themselves.

The most striking feature of the Guadalcanal campaign was that neither side had anticipated a struggle so long and severe. Neither, for various reasons, had committed enough resources at the beginning to have a decisive effect. In the end, the price of one airfield ran high.

The United States lost two aircraft carriers, seven cruisers, and fourteen destroyers, a force of ships as powerful as any she had been able to muster at any one time in the South Pacific during most of the campaign. In addition, she lost the use of other ships for varying periods because of battle damage.

Japan failed to bring in ground forces rapidly enough when she still had access to the sea approaches to the island. She never enjoyed superiority on the ground, yet her loss in dead and missing alone (twenty-four thousand), when all was over, exceeded the entire strength (twenty-three thousand) the Americans had reached at the end of the first two months. It was a small show in terms of later American operations, but it was no less intense and exhausting for those who took part.

When the Japanese attacked Pearl Harbor on December 7, 1941, they had expected to be able to consolidate their Southeast Asian conquests so rapidly that the United States and her allies, involved in Europe, would accept the new order rather than face the cost of restoring the old. With the exception of the delay caused by the stubborn resistance of MacArthur's troops in the Philippines, the Japanese program of expansion ran smoothly. The Philippines, East Indies, Malaya, Thailand, and Burma were all added to the Emperor's domain by May, 1942. Americans, British, Dutch, and Australians, unable to stop the tidal wave, were thrown back as far as India and Australia.

American positions at Guam and Wake Island were quickly smothered and most of the Pacific north of the equator and west of the 180th meridian became a Japanese ocean. South of the equator there remained a vulnerable line of communications between Hawaii and Australia, running through Samoa, the Fijis, and New Caledonia. There also remained most of a huge ninety-degree crescent of large and small islands, extending clockwise from New Guinea in the north through the Bismarcks, Solomons, and New Hebrides to New Caledonia, lying like distant outposts off the Australian shore.

Australia was a logical base for any Allied move to recover the conquered territories. It was too large for the Japanese to occupy in force. They might, however, deny its use to the Allies by cutting off its one feasible supply line, that coming in from eastward. To do this, they had to dominate the island crescent. From its western extremity they could threaten Australia directly. From its eastern extremity they could threaten the line of supply and possibly move on to capture the Fijis and Samoa, which would isolate Australia almost completely.

On January 23, 1942, the Japanese took an initial step in this direction by occupying Rabaul on New Britain Island in the Bismarck group. Rabaul had an excellent harbor and airfield sites. From Rabaul west to New Guinea and southeast through the length of the Solomons there was not a stretch of water so wide between islands that it could not be crossed by fighter aircraft. From Rabaul it would be possible to advance along the crescent in a series of steps under continuous air cover. The Japanese main base at Truk, 640 miles north, could send quick support by air or sea. More support could be channeled through bases in the Palau Islands, 1,170 miles northwest. Rabaul was the obvious starting point for a drive to isolate Australia.

Virtually unopposed, the Japanese spread out from Rabaul. First they occupied Gasmata on the south coast of New Britain. In March they hopped to New Guinea, taking Lae and Salamaua on the north side of the Papuan peninsula. This move was in the direction of Port Moresby, which was within bombing range of most of northeast Australia.

In the same month they moved in the opposite direction occupying points on Buka, Bougainville, and Shortland, all in the upper Solomons. Early in May they made a long jump down the Solomon chain to Tulagi, where they established a small seaplane base. With this addition they would be able to keep most of the island crescent under aerial surveillance. At the same time they began an amphibious expedition for the capture of Port Moresby, but broke off when its passage was threatened in the Battle of the Coral Sea.

Checked only temporarily, the Japanese turned to the North Pacific, seeking to extend their power there beyond the 180th meridian. They landed unopposed in the Aleutians in early June. At the same time, however, they were defeated in a decisive naval battle at Midway Island.

Until Midway, United States forces could only react to Japanese initiative. The Americans had been strictly on the defensive. Losses and damage at Pearl Harbor and thereafter had slashed U.S. naval strength. More important, the government had made a basic decision in January 1942 to limit military strength in the Pacific. The decision was to go on the defensive in the Pacific while assembling massive forces for the defeat of Germany in Europe. Only when that had been accomplished would the full weight of America and her allies be thrown against Japan. Combat ships, transports, aircraft, troops, and supplies of all kinds would be short in the Pacific for months to come.

The stunning Japanese loss at Midway—in which four carriers with all their planes and pilots went to the bottom—provided the United States with an opportunity that demanded action. It was essential to seize and hold the initiative while the Emperor's forces were still off balance, to strike, even if the operations had to be limited. Further, the Japanese advance eastward along the island crescent, so far unopposed, had to be stopped to protect the Australian life line.

Admiral Ernest J. King, Chief of Naval Operations, advocated the move long before Midway. After considerable debate in Washington and in the field, the Joint Chiefs of Staff issued an order on July 2 which directed the launching of a three-task assault ending in the capture of Rabaul and the expulsion of the Japanese from the islands.

Task I was the capture and occupation of Tulagi and the occupation of positions in the Santa Cruz Islands, next in the chain southeast of the Solomons. This operation was placed under the direction of the Commander, South Pacific Force, Vice Admiral Robert L. Ghormley, USN, whose headquarters were at Noumea, New Caledonia.

Task II was a drive into the western end of the Solomons, and Task III was the capture of Rabaul. Both of these efforts were to be directed by the Commander, Allied Forces, Southwest Pacific Area, General Douglas MacArthur, USA, whose headquarters were in Australia. The three missions were to be carried out consecutively; the second and third each depended on the outcome of the preceding task.

The order came as no surprise. A certain amount of planning had already been undertaken at both headquarters. It was enough to convince Ghormley and MacArthur that the chances of success were seriously threatened by continuing shortages of troops, aircraft, and shipping. Both commanders recommended that Task I be delayed until the shortages were less acute. But the Joint Chiefs saw little early improvement in the logistics situation. They were acutely aware of the advantages of moving fast; they preferred to accept the risks involved in prompt action. The Joint Chiefs were right but the decision added to the problems of the commanders in the field.

In war, the action seldom proceeds according to plan. A perfect plan reflects complete understanding of the conditions at the scene of action, of the enemy, his strengths and weaknesses, his possible courses of action, of one's own strengths and weaknesses; and in light of all these considerations lays down one's own best course of action. Because it is seldom possible to gather and correctly interpret all the relevant facts and because plain luck usually takes a hand, the action that follows may have little relation to the original plan. This is even more likely when the plan must be prepared in a hurry.

Such was the case when the execution of Task I was launched on August 7. The bulk of the First Marine Division landed east of Lunga Point on the island of Guadalcanal, an objective not originally included in that task. The attack was aimed at the airfield the Japanese had recently started building in the Lunga area. The remainder of the Marine effort was directed at Tulagi, twenty miles away. The occupation of the Santa Cruz Islands, also part of Task I, never was attempted.

The initial objectives were soon taken but the Japanese struck back hard. In the first two days enemy bombers attacked three times. They destroyed one transport and seriously delayed the unloading of the rest. The Americans still needed several days to finish the job. (It was the first amphibious action by U.S. forces in this war and lacked the polish displayed later.) The captured airfield was not yet ready for use. Nevertheless, the supporting carriers were withdrawn from continued exposure to shore-based bombers. Now the operation had to go on completely without air cover.

The most unforeseen event in the American plan, however, was the Battle of Savo Island. With the transports still unloading at Tulagi and the Lunga beachhead on the night of August 8–9, a force of cruisers and destroyers was posted to guard their western flank. Enemy ships attempting to come from that direction would have to enter the sound between Guadalcanal and Florida islands, passing either to north or south of Savo, a small island which divided the avenue of approach into north and south entrances.

Three U.S. cruisers, *Vincennes, Quincy,* and *Astoria,* and two U.S. destroyers, *Helm* and *Wilson,* covered the entrance north of Savo. Australian cruisers *Australia* and *Canberra,* and U.S. cruiser *Chicago* with U.S. destroyers *Patterson* and *Bagley* guarded the southern entrance. The two Australians were on loan from the Southwest Pacific Command. Destroyers *Ralph Talbot* and *Blue* were stationed a few miles to westward of the north and south entrances, respectively, to give early warning of approaching danger.

Guarding the western flank of the transports was a good precaution. It worked, even if only by accident. That night—it was actually 1:30 the next morning—a force of seven Japanese cruisers and one destroyer came in at high speed in a column from the west, unsuspected and undetected. Their lookouts sighted *Blue,* which failed not only to sight them but to detect them on its radar. Unannounced, the Japanese ships steamed swiftly through the south entrance. There they sighted the Southern Group, minus *Australia,* which had earlier been ordered to the anchorage at Lunga twenty miles away.

Launching torpedoes, the Japanese continued to close. Their background was darkened by a heavy rain cloud which made them more difficult to see. As their torpedoes hit, they opened fire with their guns.

Canberra, hit hard by shell and torpedo, lost all power at once and erupted in flames. Eventually she had to be abandoned and sunk. *Chicago,* with part of her bow blown off, was left behind by the speeding enemy column. *Patterson* and *Bagley* were rapidly outdistanced. A few hasty shots, none of which hit, were all the opposition the Southern Group could offer. The whole action was completed in six minutes. Now the sharp-eyed enemy, sighting the Northern Group, turned toward the new target.

Seconds before the Japanese opened fire on the Southern Group, *Patterson* had sighted them and had sounded the alarm by radio. At the same time, a Japanese float plane, launched some time earlier from one of their cruisers, located the transports at the Lunga anchorage and lighted them with a string of flares visible for miles. By now, the ships of the Northern Group should have been thoroughly alerted by radio, flares, and the gunfire to the south.

Nevertheless, when the Japanese opened fire upon them seven minutes later, the ships of Northern Group were not ready. One warship did not even have her guns trained out. The result was catastrophic. Picking up the range at first with the aid of searchlights, the Japanese were soon able to turn them off. By this time, their targets remained brilliantly lighted by fires topside which grew rapidly unmanageable as more projectiles crashed down on them. Exploding ammunition, flying debris, and flames multiplied the carnage aboard the American cruisers.

Soon all were in desperate condition—unable to shoot back at all. *Quincy* sank within forty-five minutes, *Vincennes* within an hour. *Astoria,* a burning shambles, was kept afloat until the next day. Destroyers *Helm* and *Wilson* were disregarded by the enemy, but in the darkness and confusion they were unable to help the cruisers.

The second half of the battle was over in thirty minutes. There could be nothing but a disorganized remnant in the rear of the Japanese if they should now choose to attack the nearly defenseless transports a few miles away. If those ships, so precious to the U.S. war effort in the Pacific, had been destroyed, the whole American plan culminating in the capture of Rabaul would have been stalled. It was a huge stroke of luck for the United States that Rear Admiral Gunichi Mikawa elected to pass up what should really have been the main business of his visit.

Instead, he headed back toward Rabaul with wide-open throttle, leaving the transports untouched. His own force had become scattered in the action and required time to reassemble. He was uncertain about the strength and location of any American opposition that might remain. Above all, he did not know that American aircraft would not attack him at daylight four hours later. Nevertheless, the destruction of the transports would have been worth the loss of some of his ships.

It can be argued that the U.S. ships at Savo performed their mission of protecting the transports. But the argument impressed nobody in the South Pacific. The fact was that the U.S. Navy had been surprised for reasons hard to justify. The transports were saved only by a faulty Japanese decision. The Allied losses in ships sunk and badly damaged were extreme. In contrast the Japanese suffered only superficial damage. In men the United States lost 939 killed and 654 wounded, and aboard *Canberra* the Australians lost another 84 and 55. Japanese personnel losses were small. It was the worst defeat ever suffered by the U.S. Navy. The gloom which the battles of the Coral Sea and Midway had dispelled descended once again.

The enemy had used his guns and torpedoes with skill. He was a formidable night fighter. He had employed telescope and binocular to better effect than the Americans had used their radar, an advantage the Japanese ships did not have. The implications of the battle were clear: The enemy would certainly try to take advantage of his apparent superiority at night. More important, the war in the South Pacific would continue to be hard and uncertain.

In spite of the danger of air attack, the transports continued unloading at Tulagi and Lunga until the next afternoon. They departed before dark to avoid the chance of another night visit by enemy warships. They did not return at daylight because of lack of air cover. Still on board was material sorely needed ashore, no way of safely landing it immediately in sight.

The Marines on Tulagi and Guadalcanal were now very much alone, their stocks of food, ammunition, and other essentials dangerously low. The Japanese in the Guadalcanal jungle beyond the small American enclave would certainly be reinforced. Suddenly plans had been overtaken by events. The invaders had become the besieged.

The siege intensified. During the next two months the fight for Henderson Field, as the site was named by the Marines,* assumed a typical pattern—a succession of bombardments from sea and air, dogfights high in the sky, jungle ambushes, and nights lighted by burning ships offshore.

Near the end of August American and Japanese carriers fought a

* For Major Lofton R. Henderson, USMC, shot down while leading a group of dive bombers in an attack upon one of the Japanese carriers at the Battle of Midway.

long-range battle. Surrounding geographical features acquired new names such as Bloody Ridge, the Slot, and Ironbottom Bay.* The nighttime movement of Japanese warships bringing support for their ground forces and punishment for Henderson Field was called the Tokyo Express. The name came perhaps from the regularity with which the run was made, or perhaps because of the large-caliber projectiles sometimes sent flying over the defenders with the thunderous chugging of an express train. During all of this, the Marines were holed up in an area that extended along the shore at Lunga for five or six miles and inland for varying distances up to three miles. Within this perimeter lay Henderson, its garrison battered by land, sea, and air, its line of supplies frequently cut.

The Marines' job was to secure the site they had captured, complete the field, and put it in operation. Because most of their construction equipment was not unloaded in the original assault, they were forced to expend an inordinate amount of hand labor on the field, even though they had captured some Japanese machinery. Despite these conditions, the Marines had done much. Even before a part of the Sixth Seabee Battalion arrived on September 1 to take over construction, Marine engineers had completed a facility providing a place for a limited number of small planes to take off, land, and park.

The strip, however, was no modern airdrome; there were inconveniences. Sometimes the planes stuck in the mud while trying to take off after a downpour. Sometimes landing gear was damaged while bouncing through bomb craters. Sometimes planes were destroyed completely by a shelling or a bombing.

Added to this was a chronic shortage of fuel. One day the few operating aircraft were gassed only by siphoning out the fuel remaining in other planes unfit to fly. At first there were no repair shops or other airfield installations. Barracks for air crews and service personnel were nonexistent though everyone had a foxhole. A handful of Army, Navy, and Marine Corps dive bombers and fighters were the stalwart beginning of Henderson's capability to take a hand in its own defense. Several months went by, however, before heavy bombers could be supported on a regular basis.

* More correctly a sound, and so designated today.

The Marines concentrated their ground effort on establishing a tight defense around the field. Their objective, their numbers, and the precarious state of their supply system combined to force them into a basically defensive posture.

On September 18 several transports slipped in during daylight to deliver forty-two hundred more men and a large quantity of rations and ammunition. One result of this much needed replenishment was the resumption of three meals a day. Even with captured Japanese rice, shortages had limited the defenders to two meals a day for most of the time since their landing.

By October 10 they had fought two successful defensive actions and some minor offensive skirmishes. They had fought well, but their prospects depended upon a continuing flow of reinforcements and supplies and upon the denial of similar support to the enemy. The outlook in this direction was not bright.

The sea approaches to Guadalcanal, across which each adversary's supply lines extended, had become a no man's land where the submarines and aircraft of each side struck without warning. Both sides faced difficulties in crossing this area, but the Japanese seemed to be overcoming their problems more effectively. They used destroyers and sometimes cruisers as transports, making use of their high speed and the cover of darkness to land reinforcements and supplies almost at will. Although these ships, built for other purposes, had only limited capacity as transports, the Japanese had relatively large numbers of them in the South Pacific. For the carrier battle of the eastern Solomons on August 23–25, for example, Japan assembled 17 cruisers and 34 destroyers. In contrast, the United States was able to muster only 7 cruisers and 17 destroyers.

Earlier U.S. losses accounted in part for the ship shortage, but the prime reason was the United States' Europe-first policy. Already a powerful escort was being assembled on the U.S. east coast for the North African invasion and many destroyers had for months been on the job of protecting convoys against German submarines in the Atlantic. Only the limited resources left after these requirements were met could go to the Pacific. The Guadalcanal offensive had been launched as a calculated risk. Now the wisdom of that risk was in question.

In late August the Marines brought in SBDs—Douglas Dauntless dive bombers—to operate from Henderson Field, and these dictated the peculiar kind of warfare that was now fought offshore. They were augmented from time to time by similar Navy squadrons from disabled carriers.

The SBD was light and rugged enough to survive the inhospitable surface of Henderson Field. It was the principal means of carrying the air attack to Japanese shipping. The SBD could fly a distance of two hundred miles, strike, and return. At that range it had to find the target promptly or risk the possibility of running out of fuel. It was not equipped with radar. Though aircraft occasionally went up at night, the field had no facilities for regular night operations.

Thus the Japanese soon discovered that while it was unsafe for their ships to steam within two hundred miles of Henderson Field during daylight, it was not a particularly dangerous thing to do at night. The night lasts long enough in that latitude to permit a thirty-three-knot ship to run the two hundred miles, unload a limited cargo, and race back outside the limit again with only a little daylight exposure.

It was this combination of circumstances that gave birth to the Tokyo Express. Crossing into the danger zone a little before dark, and running at full power, a night's express of several fast Japanese ships reached the beaches at the west end of the island about midnight. Men, munitions, and supplies were hastily unloaded into small craft sent out from shore. Then the ships would turn back, throttles wide open once more, reaching the safety of the two-hundred-mile mark a little after daylight. Here they would slow to an easier pace for the rest of the run back to base. Sometimes, while the others were unloading, one or more of these ships would slip the few miles down the Guadalcanal coast and shell the American airfield. The shelling caused the Americans loss of sleep and sometimes casualties that had pronounced effects on the next morning's air operations.

The Americans brought in their support during the day. They had a minimum of conventional transports with no hope of early replacement of losses. The North African invasion had first priority. The fighter aircraft at Guadalcanal did a magnificent job considering the difficulties under which they worked but Japanese planes sometimes got through the air defenses. Anchored transports made easy targets for submarines. And finally, it took many hours to unload by the primitive means available.

Like the Japanese, the Americans were also forced to improvise. With the first trace of daylight, perhaps after a thunderous night of shelling, a converted U.S. destroyer dating from World War One might glide into the Lunga anchorage and drop anchor. The sea watch would then remain on station with several men standing ready on the forecastle to slip the chain for an emergency getaway. The ship's cargo might include a deck load of bombs and drums of aviation gas. The bombs were transferred to barges brought out from shore. The gasoline drums were pushed overboard, where they floated on the smooth surface until utility boats rounded them up with cargo nets and hauled them slowly through the water to the beach.

The old destroyer would depart as soon as her driblet of supplies was unloaded. Gas was a chronic problem. A submarine brought a cargo of the barreled fuel one day. On another, under conditions of extreme crisis, Marine transport aircraft flew it in. The methods used by both sides were those of blockade-runners. The Guadalcanal campaign had deteriorated into a strangulation contest.

The Americans did not have enough land-based bombers to attack Japanese bases at Rabaul and the upper Solomons on a steady basis. Neither did they have enough carriers and submarines to threaten seriously the enemy's sea lanes beyond reach of the Guadalcanal-based aircraft. There was only one way to end the precarious stalemate which had set in: The Tokyo Express must be stopped before it broke the stalemate itself by speeding up the flow of troops and supplies to the Japanese. American ships, badly defeated in one night engagement, would have to meet the enemy at night again, and as often as necessary, to stop the Express and save Henderson Field.

Task Group 64.2, pushing toward Guadalcanal on the late afternoon of Sunday, October 11, was going in.

Chapter Two

BATTLE STATIONS

LESS THAN THREE WEEKS before this Sunday in October, the Commander, South Pacific Force—Comsopac—had established a "Screening and Attack Force" of six cruisers and nine destroyers. The name of the force provided a good description of its mission. Following standard procedure it was assigned a numerical designator—64.

Because of the ship shortage, commanders seldom saw all of their ships at any one time. Comsopac was forever temporarily taking a cruiser here, a destroyer there, to fill a spot made vacant somewhere else by enemy action or some other unforeseen development. Task Force 64 was no exception; it was subject to the same sort of improvisation. October 11 Admiral Scott, commander of the new Task Force 64, was out with four rather than six cruisers and only five of his destroyers. To pinpoint this latest group in his communications, he called it Task Group 64.2.

Sunset caused no change in the steady advance of the ships. The arrow continued to point to the northwest. Silhouetted against the western sky, the ships forming the arrow showed marked differences. Even beyond these, there were important invisible differences. Ships are sailed by men, and a ship usually acquires a personality that, to a degree, is a composite of all the personalities on board. But in the final analysis, a ship's personality most nearly reflects that of its captain. The captain's attitudes, however indirectly expressed, prompt similar attitudes at every level in the command. Thanks to the way in which a ship's company is organized and governed, the captain's influence is decisive. The morale, the fighting spirit of his command, is his to make or break.

Even physically no two of the cruisers in Task Group 64.2 were completely alike. *San Francisco* was a "heavy"; her main battery con-

16

sisted of nine 8-inch guns mounted in three turrets, two forward and one aft. Her skipper was Captain Charles H. McMorris. *Boise,* commanded by Captain Edward J. Moran, was a light cruiser. The significant point of distinction between "light" and "heavy" cruisers lay in the size of their main battery guns rather than in their displacements. *Boise's* main battery guns were 6-inch; she mounted a total of fifteen distributed in five three-gun turrets, three forward and two aft.

Salt Lake City, third in column, was commanded by Captain Ernest G. Small. She was another heavy cruiser, a handsome ship with clipper bow, raked stacks and masts, and long, low hull lines. She mounted ten 8-inch guns, five distributed two–three in two turrents forward and another five similarly distributed aft. Last in column was *Helena,* commanded by Captain Gilbert C. Hoover. Another "light," her main battery of fifteen 6-inch guns was distributed like *Boise's.* She resembled *Boise* in most other respects, too.

All of the cruisers were studded with dual-purpose (surface and air target) 5-inch batteries known as the secondary or antiaircraft batteries, plus numerous heavy machine guns. They also carried up to four seaplanes for antisubmarine patrol, scouting, and gunfire observation. Each cruiser with its load of fuel, ammunition, stores, and men displaced twelve to thirteen thousand tons. Unlike Japanese cruisers, none of the U.S. ships was equipped with torpedoes. The assumption of the designers seems to have been that since the cruisers' guns could reach so far, they would seldom become engaged at the shorter torpedo ranges.

The destroyers in the antisubmarine screen displaced about two thousand tons. They belonged to Squadron Twelve. Each carried a battery of four dual-purpose 5-inch guns in separate, enclosed mounts, plus several heavy machine guns, a single bank of five 21-inch torpedo tubes which could be aimed to either side, and several depth-charge launchers.

Uncomfortable, particularly in rough weather, the destroyer was nevertheless a preferred type of surface ship duty. The "Old Man" was usually in his thirties and the other officers and petty officers, like him, were filling more responsible positions than they could have expected to hold in larger ships.

Captain Robert G. Tobin, commander of the squadron, was in

Farenholt. The individual destroyer skippers were Eugene T. Seaward of *Farenholt,* Edmund B. Taylor of *Duncan,* William E. Hank of *Laffey,* Ralph E. Wilson of *Buchanan,* and William G. Cooper of *Mc-Calla.* All were lieutenant commanders except Wilson, who had recently been promoted to commander.

The ships' silhouettes faded with the short tropical twilight. A slender new moon, low in the west, would soon follow the sun. The ships showed no lights and soon became dark shadows which could be found only one or two at a time in the limited field of a pair of binoculars. The moment anticipated in Scott's orders was approaching. It had been heralded some hours before.

Early that morning a B-17 from Colonel LaVerne G. Saunders' Eleventh Bombardment Group, U.S. Army Air Forces, had taken off on a reconnaissance flight from its base at Espiritu Santo, in the New Hebrides Islands. At 10:30 and eight hundred miles to the northwest, while approaching the east end of Bougainville, the B-17 crew made a sighting. What appeared to be two cruisers and six destroyers were heading down the Slot toward Guadalcanal, 260 miles away. The ships were steaming at an estimated speed of twenty-five knots. The B-17 pilot alerted Henderson Field by radio. The alarm was then relayed to the forces afloat, including Task Group 64.2.

During the noon hour that same day the radar at Henderson Field picked up two flights of unidentified planes 138 miles out in the direction of Rabaul. Apparently they had eluded the Coast Watchers. Army, Navy, and Marine pilots hastily scrambled fifty-one fighters of various kinds. A few other aircraft in exposed positions around the field took off to fly in circles at a safe distance until the alert was over.

The field was hardly cleared before the attack came in—sixteen Zero fighters followed by two groups of eighteen and sixteen twin-engine bombers, followed by thirteen more Zeros. They were flying high, and lack of high-altitude oxygen equipment prevented the Army P-39s from reaching them.

The action was fast, in fact it was over before some of the Marine and Navy fighters could join. Those who reached high altitude in time to meet the enemy worked with the skill which a tour of duty at Henderson Field so quickly developed. But in the hot stillness on the ground men crouching in foxholes could hear only a remote hum, like the confused buzzing of a hive of bees. Four U.S. fighters were lost, but one of the pilots was rescued offshore by a utility boat. The defense spoiled the aim of the Japanese bombers so effectively that they overshot the target. All their bombs crashed harmlessly into the surrounding jungle.

Despite this interruption, the departure of routine patrols from Henderson Field was not greatly delayed. At 2:45 P.M. Lieutenant (jg) H. N. Murphy of the Navy and Staff Sergeant H. Bruce of the Marines rediscovered the B-17's contact. Two hundred and ten miles out in the direction from which the bombers had come was a formation of eight enemy ships. They were passing through a point in the Slot between Kolambangara and Choiseul islands, steering for Guadalcanal. Six destroyers formed an oval on the blue surface of the water enclosing two larger ships which steamed in column. Over them circled a protective flight of several Zeros. Henderson flashed a message to all commands, including all USN ships, in uncoded language: "6 DDs 2 cruisers bearing 305 distance 210 from Guadalcanal course 120."

If this were another Tokyo Express run, why did it start out so early that it needed air cover? If these were all fast ships, as the contact reports indicated, why did they not wait until dusk to cross the two-hundred-mile mark? At the field these matters were academic.

Whatever the Japanese were up to, it was impossible now to get a strike armed and off in time to return before dark. Major General Roy S. Geiger, USMC, commanding all air operations at Guadalcanal, decided not to risk further reducing his already limited resources in a mass nighttime landing of weary pilots and battle-damaged aircraft. This time, with U.S. warships moving into position, he hoped there would be other means of stopping the enemy. Reconnaissance continued. At sunset the eight ships were only one hundred and ten miles away.

A report of the last sighting probably reached Scott, but the first two were enough. The enemy force could reach Guadalcanal long before midnight. For two days Scott had been cruising south and east of the island waiting for something like this. The timing of his mission was set to coincide with the movement of two transports from Nou-

mea bringing the first of the Army troops who were eventually to re-
lieve the First Marine Division. They were due on the thirteenth. He
had been placed in position both to screen the U.S. support effort and
to attack the enemy's. A submarine might see him at any time, but he
could avoid some air reconnaissance by remaining beyond the range
of the enemy's scouting aircraft for a maximum length of time each
day.

Daily at noon he left this sanctuary and started in at good speed to
reach the vicinity of Savo Island and a possible encounter by 11 P.M.
On the ninth and tenth he had gone through these motions but had
turned back after dark because there were no contact reports. Today,
well before sunset, he had signaled his ships: "We are going in. Jap
force believed to be two cruisers and six DDs."

The moon set an hour after the sun. The stars did little to light the
darkness. The men were already at battle stations gazing out at the
crowding black void. Scott was not going to repeat one mistake made
by the Americans at the Battle of Savo Island. He was ready to shoot
before there was even the slightest possibility of running into the
enemy. He had sent all hands to battle stations at sundown.

U.S. cruisers and destroyers were all about ten times longer than
they were wide. Inside, they were divided into many watertight compartments, some large, some small, like deep ice cube trays having
several grids with random divisions stacked one upon the other.
There were battle stations in many of the compartments. Men were
present at these to perform tasks which were necessary, or might become necessary, in battle. Most of these tasks involved the operation
of some kind of machinery or apparatus. There were many men at the
guns, searchlights, torpedoes, and on the bridge and other places topside. The majority, however, had stations below decks. This was true
even of the gunnery department, which had a large number of men in
the magazines and at other points along the ammunition trains.

A long wait for a battle in a closed compartment was tedious and
disquieting. When the shooting finally started some men would be released from the misery of inaction. Gun crews and ammunition
passers would spring into furious activity which took all their attention. But many more men would simply wait as the ship vibrated with
the shock of its own gunfire. Their release—if it came—would be sig-

naled only by the jolting blow of a torpedo or the rending explosion of a shell inside their own ship.

Suddenly they would be required to quell the horrors of fire and flooding and human injury for which the best training could hardly prepare them. Their attitude toward the enemy was conditioned by their situation. They never saw him. He was not an antagonist with whom they squared off, matching cunning, strength, and skill. Below decks, the enemy was an impersonal phenomenon like the weather, like a hurricane.

These ships carried several weapons; the oldest and most common was the gun. Despite eighty years of continuing effort to develop armor that could stop progressively bigger projectiles, the gun seldom lost its advantage. Tougher, thicker armor led to heavier, faster projectiles with harder noses and delayed action fuses fired from larger, more accurate guns. An 8-inch shell could penetrate about eight inches of armor at a favorable angle of impact. While it would have been possible to stop the most destructive shell if the armor had been tough and thick enough, the armor's excessive weight would have imposed unacceptable limitations on other equipment that a warship carried. The result of this was a compromise and something less than perfect protection against gunfire.

In battleships the thickest armor protected only the more vital areas. Other areas had less. In cruisers the arrangement of armor was the same, but the thickness was much less. Armor was nearly nonexistent in destroyers.

Of Scott's ships, the only one that had ever received serious damage was *Helena*. In the first two minutes of the Japanese raid at Pearl Harbor, ten months earlier, she had been struck by an aircraft torpedo. It tore a hole at the turn of the bilge in the forward engine room, a hole forty feet long and high enough at the middle for a man to stand in. The twenty-two-ton reduction gear of Number One Main Engine was uprooted and flung over on its side. The two turbine shafts and the propeller shaft were parted at the flanges. Ninety were killed or injured in the blast which penetrated the spaces above the engine room through doors and hatches, kept open for men still hurrying to their battle stations. It had taken six months to repair the damage.

While *Helena* underwent repairs, the other three cruisers now in

Task Group 64.2 had steamed thousands of miles escorting transports and supporting carriers during their operations. *San Francisco* and *Salt Lake City* had fought off enemy aircraft more than once, and *Salt Lake City* had bombarded enemy shore positions in the Marshalls.

The four were now working together for the first time. At the outbreak of the war, each had belonged to a different division. At that time, the assignment of ships to divisions was based on their similarity of characteristics. This system was still desirable, but no longer possible. Losses, time out for repairs, and urgent missions forced the indiscriminate mixing of cruisers, new and old, light and heavy.

The latest of the cruisers in Task Group 64.2, *Helena* had been in commission for two years. Men had been transferred from all the cruisers to provide a nucleus for vessels just entering service, but there still remained a solid backbone of experience in all four ships.

The destroyers of Task Group 64.2 were all new. They had been assigned to Squadron Twelve before they left home waters. They had arrived in the South Pacific, however, one at a time over the previous two months and had been sent immediately to commands requiring destroyers—any destroyers.

Now they were assembled as a squadron for the first time although, in fact, four were still missing. Except for the majority of officers and petty officers, their crews were novices at sea. Under the pressures of wartime demands, their training had been fast and abbreviated; the ships had been rushed to the combat area with a minimum of gun, torpedo, and depth-charge practice. The strenuous efforts of their captains notwithstanding, the destroyer crews were still green by all objective standards.

In fact, Scott was approaching a battle in command of a hurriedly gathered task group whose captains were largely unknown to him either personally or through observing the performance of their commands. There had been only a brief opportunity at Espiritu Santo to get acquainted before the present mission. Yet this mission surely would include fighting under conditions with which the modern U.S. Navy had had no experience beyond the gallant, outclassed effort of the Asiatic Fleet in the first months of war, the debacle at Savo Island, and an inadequate amount of peacetime drill.

There was time for only some conferences, a little gunnery practice, a little maneuvering as a group. This was hardly enough. Only a longer period of experience together could possibly establish the mutual understanding and confidence required to make a team. In many respects Task Group 64.2 on October 11 was an unknown quantity, both to its commander and to its captains.

This lack of familiarity was aggravated insofar as the use of radar was concerned. Radar at this time was still in the development stage; it was still emerging from the laboratory. It was not yet a practical device in wide use. Its principle had been known to the international scientific community for years. As early as 1886 the German Heinrich Hertz had demonstrated that radio waves were reflected by solid objects. By 1904 patents had been granted by several governments for schemes exploiting this property. Nothing, however, came of them. Finally in the 1930's efforts to apply the principle were stepped up by several nations trying to use it for military purposes. The assured role of aircraft in future warfare made the development of defenses urgent. Radar was certainly one obvious defense, and the United States Army and Navy were both active in radar research.

In 1934 the Navy developed an idea for applying Hertz's principle in a mobile vehicle such as a ship or an airplane. A transmitter fired a quick burst of radio waves from an antenna aimed in an exact direction. It was like the flight of a short squirt of water from a garden hose. If there was a solid object in the line of fire, the waves bounced off and returned to the antenna as an echo. Their return was registered in a receiver connected to the same antenna.

The outgoing bursts or pulses were timed so that the echoes could be compared with the pulses that originated them. Comparison showed the difference in time between the departure of the pulse and the return of its echo. The speed with which the waves traveled was known, so distance to the object was indicated by this time difference.

The first test of a radar aboard ship took place in December, 1938. An immense 17-foot-square "bedspring" antenna was installed on the old battleship *New York*. It could detect objects in the air, on the surface of the water, and ashore. It could even follow the flight of the ship's own 14-inch projectiles. Equipment embodying some of the findings of this test was installed in a battleship, a carrier, and three cruisers in May, 1940. Improved models, designed for more specific applications, followed rapidly. By October, 1942, there were few U.S. combat ships without some kind of radar.

Great Britain and the United States led their opponents in the development of the new device. There was no evidence yet that the Japanese had put it into service. One great advantage it provided was the ability to "see" in a night engagement when the enemy could not. Still, radar had not helped at the Battle of Savo Island.

Radar had disadvantages, too. One was the complex nature of the apparatus. It was much more sophisticated than the ordinary radio transmitter and receiver. Special training was required to qualify men who could keep it in repair. The training took time, and some ships were still without the men. Added to this, radar was a very recent entry in the Navy supply system. The experience needed to establish a reasonably accurate spare-parts program was still being accumulated. Consequently sets were frequently out of order for lack of proper maintenance, or spare parts, or both.

Even with a set in good repair, training was also needed to use it properly. Most radars at this time had two windows, or "scopes," from which the operator got his information. The first scope showed the direction of the target. This was simple enough. The second, however, contained a picture that looked like a ground-level view of a field of waving grass. Like blades of grass, a series of luminous vertical green lines danced up and down. When the radar was aimed at an object, a trained operator would see a dot or "pip" within this agitation and could single it out by twisting a knob. The distance to the object was then read from a scale attached to the knob.

The art of finding a pip, and of recognizing a false pip, was called pipology. It was hard to master. Captains were frequently summoned from their bunks at night, guns alerted, and occasionally a ship's company sent to battle stations because of a false pip. Real targets sometimes slipped by undetected. Few ships had enough trained operators.

With several targets present, the "pip and grass" type of radar suffered a serious limitation. It could look in only one direction at a time. Between consecutive looks, the same target might have moved enough to make it hard to find again and hard to keep identified among other moving targets. Procedures to overcome this difficulty were established, but they were laborious and uncertain at best.

Finally, the target information obtained by radar had to be conveyed to the bridge to be acted upon. At this time, the only means of conveying it rapidly enough in battle was the telephone and never was the old saying, "One picture is worth ten thousand words," truer. It took an experienced officer to relay the right word effectively.

All ships in Task Group 64.2 had gunnery radars, a superior substitute for optical equipment in getting the guns on target, particularly at night. While the narrow beam of waves they emitted, excellent for gunnery, made them poor searchers, they could be and were used in that capacity. All of the cruisers had the SC search radar, used for both air and surface detection. *Helena* and *Boise,* having both been home lately, also had the SG, the new surface-search radar. This version could reach farther out on the surface and had an important feature which overcame the "pip and grass" limitations of the SC. In a scope like a television screen it displayed a diagram of luminous dots representing in number and relative position all the objects within its range in every direction. If the objects were moving, the dots moved on the screen. Their distance and direction could be picked off directly. The picture still had to be conveyed to the bridge by imperfect means, but at the set it was complete, accurate, and continuous.

Despite her lack of the latest radar gear, Scott chose *San Francisco* for his flagship rather than the better equipped *Helena* or *Boise.* In the rapid and highly classified development of radar at this time, most commanders were uninformed of capabilities newly placed at their disposal—a glaring example of too much secrecy. Captain Hoover of *Helena* did not urge Scott to change his decision nor, in all probability, did Captain Moran of *Boise.* Neither was in a position to argue that *San Francisco* could not achieve adequate results with her older equipment. Skillful operators could do much to close the gap caused by differences in design. Besides, little was known in any ship of the radar capabilities of the others. This was one of the more serious deficiencies arising from the urgency with which the screening and attack force was assembled and committed.

By 8:30 P.M. the task group was off Cape Hunter, the southwest corner of Guadalcanal. From here the beach ran northwest for several miles parallel to the track of the ships. The chart showed coral bordering most of this stretch, along whose irregularities appeared such names as Aowana Point, Wanderer Bay, Tangarare Mission, and Ovi Harbor. Close behind, peaks rose as high as twenty-eight hundred feet. Several dotted lines marked "trail" started at the water, cut rather too directly through the contour lines, and stopped abruptly farther inland in a large, blank area. The island was still far off, the high points just beginning to appear in the SG radar scope.

At 9:15 Scott changed course. At West Cape, farther ahead, the coast turned north. The new course would take him abreast of it, ten miles off, until he reached its northern extremity, the vicinity of Cape Esperance. This was the general neighborhood in which the enemy had been landing his reinforcements.

The probable path of the two cruisers and six destroyers he sought crossed his own twenty-five miles ahead. The enemy ships were probably near the crossing point now, heading in for the beaches unaware, he hoped, of his presence. The enemy destroyers would go close inshore to unload. The cruisers, if they carried no troops or cargo, would patrol at some distance offshore. Perhaps they would steam the short distance down the north shore to bombard Henderson Field.

Darkness is relative. The eye sees an object in the dark because it appears a little blacker than its background. If there is enough contrast, the shape of the object will be clear. Otherwise it may appear as an ill-defined shadow, or may have to be approached closer to be seen at all. On this night the visibility was variable. The moon was down and the faint illumination of the stars was diminished by patches of cloud and occasional areas of surface haze.

Most of Scott's radars were searching a zone beyond the range of the lookouts, greatly extending the sweep of their binoculars. But radar had still another disadvantage. With special counterequipment, it was possible to identify the waves given out by separate types of radar. There had been intelligence reports indicating that the Japanese might have equipment capable of spotting the transmissions of the SC. In short, they could detect the presence of U.S. ships using SC radar in their vicinity.

Whatever credit he gave this intelligence, Scott was bent upon surprise. To increase his chances of gaining this edge he was willing to give up some of his ability to search. Earlier in the evening, he had ordered the SC radars to be turned off. The gunnery radars of all ships and the SGs of *Helena* and *Boise,* however, continued in use.

Total surprise was going to be difficult to achieve under the best circumstances. Scott might have been seen earlier in the day and his intentions correctly anticipated. A trap could be waiting for him. Even if there were no trap, he would still have to find the enemy's ships before he could attack them. If they were inshore now, they would not show up well against the land background, either visually or on most radar.

On the other hand, if Scott took his whole force in for a close search, he might be ambushed from seaward, with his back against the coast. If he sent only some of his ships in to scout, he divided his strength and risked being defeated piecemeal by a concentrated enemy. Furthermore, since he did not know which beaches the Japanese were using, too much time could be wasted in searching the wrong places. And, if they were dispersed at several beaches, the first ships discovered might warn the others in time to permit their escape.

Scott decided to use the cruiser seaplanes to search, while he kept his task group concentrated at a prudent distance offshore. Two days earlier he had distributed a brief memorandum of instructions. It was a plan to the extent that the highly unpredictable nature of the mission would permit.

It described the intended manner of search, including use of aircraft and the formation and tentative track of the ships. It contained a few orders concerning methods of communication and the use of weapons, and it designated a morning rendezvous for ships which became separated in battle. It directed that TBS (voice radio) silence be maintained "as long as practicable, but any ship may use it to report contacts." It directed destroyers to "fire torpedoes at large ships and gun destroyers and small craft." One important provision, however, does not appear in the memorandum and was apparently passed orally during the conferences at Espiritu Santo, for Scott stated in his subsequent action report that "I had instructed all captains to open fire without my order when the enemy was located."

A fast-moving plane is not the ideal scout for a nighttime search of the ocean surface, particularly when looking for something stationary like an anchored ship. But the ships Task Group 64.2 was looking for would not remain anchored all night. And in the meantime the phosphorescent wake of a landing craft or an errant light, aboard or ashore, might give them away. In fact, a Japanese plane had discovered the anchored U.S. transports at the Battle of Savo Island.

Scott planned to have one plane from each cruiser scout the shoreline and search to seaward. A contact was to be reported and held, if possible, until the approach of friendly ships. The contact's position was to be indicated by float lights or even the release of bombs. Flares were to be carried but used only on order. The pilots were to land at Tulagi upon completion of the mission, returning to their ships when directed the next day.

The cruisers usually launched aircraft by catapult, though if a ship stopped in calm water planes could be put over the side with a crane. The aircraft were Curtis SOCs, biplanes with a single float and single engine. Their "skin" was "doped" fabric rather than the aluminum of later models and they were highly inflammable. They took off at about 60 knots. The catapult hurled them into the air at the same speed and eliminated the dangerous bumping involved in most water take-offs.

The catapult was a girder on a turntable which could be aimed over the side. It was about seventy feet long and was fitted with a track and car. The car was attached to a piston under the track by a heavy wire cable running over several pulleys. The piston worked in a cylinder under the pressure of expanding gases given off by the burning of a charge of powder, the same kind of powder used in the guns.

With the plane clamped down on the car at the inboard end and the engine running at full throttle, the catapult was fired by pulling a lanyard. The car would jerk forward, picking up speed until, at the other end, it reached the flying speed of the plane. There it would hit a pair of buffers and stop suddenly. The jolt released the clamps and sent the plane sailing out over the water in flight. It was a reliable system; mishaps were rare, but the possibility of serious accident was never absent.

At 9:45 Scott had only thirteen more miles to go before pulling abreast of Cape Esperance. If there were to be a fight, it would come soon.

The weather held constant, a light breeze from the southeast, a smooth sea, and a dark night of varying visibility relieved by occasional flashes of lightning on the northwest horizon, the direction of the Slot. Scott slowed to twenty-five knots and at ten o'clock he slowed again to twenty. By this time one plane in each cruiser was warmed up, manned, and ready to launch. A pilot and observer waited in each.

"Launch aircraft!" The catapult officer in *Salt Lake City* gave the signaled command by swinging a dimmed flashlight in a circle. Lieutenant William F. Tate, Jr., the pilot, opened his throttle wide. The engine roared and the plane shook as the propeller strained against the temporary bonds that held the car. Tate waited with a hand on the stick, feet on the rudder bar, his head pressed against the high back of his seat. Claude W. Morgan, first class aviation radioman, the observer, lowered his head, arms extended against the front of his cockpit, his back planted firmly against the rear.

The catapult officer waited to fire at the beginning of the up-roll. If he fired with the ship rolling the other way, the catapult would be tilted down at the water as the plane shot off. Ordinarily he watched the horizon to determine the moment to fire. But in darkness like this he had to feel the roll of the ship in the pressure of his feet on the deck to help his eyes.

The sensation of catapulting, the feeling that one's stomach is being left behind, occurs only with the jerk at the beginning of the shot. By the time the plane is flying, the muscles have relaxed.

But there was a difference this time for the two-man crew of *Salt Lake City*'s scout plane. Morgan, bent over in the rear cockpit, saw fire immediately. Hot magnesium sparks burned his ankles as the plane shot forward. He knew the source at once; it was the extra flares! They had not been stowed as they should have been. His first thought was to tell Tate, but he could not stay in his seat with the flares burning at his feet.

Following common practice in catapult shots, he had not yet fastened his parachute harness. Flipping open the safety-belt buckle, he rose with a strong impulse to jump out of the plane. Fortunately, his helmet cord, providing the radio earphone connections, was plugged in and jerked him back. In the moment required to slip off the helmet he decided on another move. With the plane boring through the black night, tail on fire, he climbed from his cockpit out onto the canopy. He crawled forward fighting against the powerful slipstream, over the forward cockpit and Tate's head, grabbing anything he could find for a hand hold. Finally, he found the handle in the upper wing just forward of the pilot. Then he groped his way down to a standing position on the lower left wing next to the fuselage and shouted, "Land! Land!"

Startled watchers in the task group saw the plane hit the water about five hundred yards abreast the cruiser column and disappear at once in its own flames. They flared for two or three minutes and then died away.

In *San Francisco* the captain's battle station was the bridge, which included the pilothouse and the open space around it. Directly below was the signal bridge where the flag bags and signal searchlights were located. This also served as the Admiral's station, or flag bridge. It, too, had been illuminated in the glare of the burning plane.

Gasoline, flares, and float lights had all fed the flames which enveloped the plane. To all observers, it seemed impossible that a man could have escaped or survived such withering heat. Scott could have sent back a destroyer to search but the chances of finding anything at all were too remote to warrant reducing his strength now.

The blaze had completely changed the situation. It must have been seen at every point along the shore to its northern extremity. Undoubtedly, it had alerted every ship that might be on that stretch of coast and far to seaward. Only if the enemy were already on the north shore, east of Cape Esperance, separated from the fire by the high ground at the northwest shoulder of the island, could he possibly have missed the signal. It had to be assumed that the advantage of surprise, if it existed before, was now lost. None of this, however, changed Scott's orders. He continued ahead.

Chapter Three

UNCERTAINTY

AT EIGHT O'CLOCK ON THE MORNING OF SUNDAY, October 11, eight Japanese warships got under way from the Shortland Island anchorage at the southeast end of the large island of Bougainville. Ahead of them was another of those over-250-mile runs in each direction for the delivery of reinforcements to Japanese troops on Guadalcanal. It should be uneventful but uncertainty was always a principal element of war.

Most, if not all, of these ships had made the run before. *Nisshin* had been down on October 3 and again on October 8. The first time she carried four 15-cm. howitzers, two field guns, three ammunition tractors, two trucks, sixteen landing craft, and 2,314 army officers and men. The cargo for the second trip was similar.

Commissioned as a seaplane carrier and even still carrying a few, she had much more room for bulky freight than cruisers or destroyers had and, with a maximum speed of about 26 knots, she was a good deal faster than the ordinary merchant ship.

No flag officer was present for this operation; *Nisshin's* captain commanded the entire force. One of the other ships, *Chitose,* was also a seaplane carrier capable of the same speed. The rest were destroyers. The untrained eye, seeing the seaplane carriers from the air, particularly when they were in company with destroyers, could mistake them for cruisers. Both were named for earlier ships of the Imperial Navy. *Nisshin* meant "Ever Advancing" and *Chitose* "A Thousand Years."

When the ships cleared the anchorage, they set course for the entrance into the Slot. They maintained an easy 15 knots. *Chitose* followed *Nisshin* at a distance of fifteen hundred yards. The six destroyers took stations around them at equal intervals on the perimeter of a large oval. Two or three of *Nisshin*'s seaplanes were launched and flew ahead and on the flanks watching for a white feather or an unnatural swirl in the water which would mark the presence of a stalking submarine.

All ships zigzagged together to make it more difficult for a submarine to reach a favorable torpedo-firing position. The destroyers, equipped with underwater listening gear and depth charges, provided further antisubmarine protection and their guns defended against possible attack by air or surface enemies.

The destroyers also carried limited numbers of troops and supplies because no means of fast transport could be overlooked in supporting the ground forces at Guadalcanal. They were *Asagumo*, meaning "Morning Cloud"; *Akizuki*, "Autumn Moon"; *Murakumo*, "Gathering Clouds"; *Natsugumo*, "Summer Cloud"; *Shirayuki*, "White Snow"; and *Yamagumo*, "Cloud Hung over the Mountains."

This Reinforcement Group, as it was called, proceeded along its track until 10:30 A.M., when an airplane was sighted and identified as a U.S. B-17. Crews went to battle stations and the ships increased speed to permit more rapid maneuvering. The plane hovered out of range for a few minutes and then departed. This kind of encounter was not very disturbing. B-17s were sometimes seen in the vicinity of the Shortland anchorage on reconnaissance. Missions commencing this early in the day could not expect to escape all observation from the air. Had this been a dive bomber like those at the enemy field at Guadalcanal it would have been different. The appearance of a dive bomber here would have indicated the possibility that a U.S. carrier was within striking range. The planes at Guadalcanal did not come this far.

At noon six land-based Zeros reported overhead to provide protection against air attack. The group was forty miles beyond the two-hundred-mile arc centered at the Guadalcanal field. After crossing this mark and until sunset the ships would be very inviting targets. They would become increasingly vulnerable as they drew closer to their destination. In addition to the combat air patrol flying overhead, the Japanese command at Rabaul had arranged for an air attack against Henderson Field at midday. This was aimed at further reducing American ability to interfere with the Reinforcement Group.

At one o'clock *Nisshin* recovered her seaplanes. At three the formation crossed the two-hundred-mile mark. They were now in no man's land. Zigzagging was discontinued and speed pushed up to maximum. This would enable the ships to reach the Guadalcanal beaches, unload, and return fast to the two-hundred-mile mark the next morning with minimum daylight exposure to enemy aircraft. Air cover would also be provided for the few vulnerable daylight hours at the end of the run. Experience indicated that the probability of trouble at the beaches was small. The hours remaining before dark this day were likely to be the most critical.

The ships plowed steadily ahead under bright skies and the languid circling of the combat air patrol. Their progress through the rest of the afternoon was unchallenged. If they saw the aerial scouts who twice sighted them and reported them back to Henderson Field, the fact went unmentioned in the report later submitted by the commanding officer of *Nisshin.*

With sunset came increased confidence. Chances of completing the mission as another routine supply run looked excellent. The combat air patrol had not been needed. If this had been known beforehand, the planes could have been saved. Now only the pilots could be saved, for the planes did not have enough fuel left to return to Buka, the nearest field, at the far end of Bougainville. This had been foreseen. The importance of getting these ships through, however, had warranted the expenditure of the six Zeros simply as insurance. Each made a "wheels up" landing in the dusk as close as possible to a destroyer. The destroyer promptly lowered a boat and recovered the pilot as his plane sank. One plane, however, overturned on hitting the water and the pilot was lost.

Maximum speed was resumed as darkness set in and at 7:40 P.M. all hands were sent to battle stations. It was simply a reasonable precaution and not the result of any new information. The Americans, so far as was known, were nowhere near. At about 9:45 P.M. the Reinforcement Group swept through the seven-mile interval between Savo Island and Cape Esperance. Then the ships dispersed and proceeded to several different beaches along the north shore of Guadalcanal. None saw any unusual glow in the sky at 10 P.M. Unloading commenced as soon as they were anchored.

Reliable communications are always essential, but in battle are often difficult to achieve. The history of warfare is riddled with examples of opportunities lost because commanders were not informed in time. Scott, approaching Cape Esperance, must give commands and receive information across stretches of water in darkness without disclosing his position.

Signals by light were out of the question. Task Group 64.2 was linked by a short-range voice radio system called TBS. This most nearly met Scott's needs but individual sets could get out of tune at the wrong moment. Furthermore, TBS transmissions could be intercepted. These would not only betray the presence of U.S. ships but would tell something of what they were doing.

Scott had therefore cautioned his captains in his instructions to keep TBS silence "as long as practicable." He had authorized its use, however, for reporting contacts. He was using it now to carry his orders to his ships. And in this connection the system had another drawback. It was like a ten-party telephone line. Everybody could talk at the same time, making it impossible to transmit orders promptly. The need for silence was obvious. It was up to individual captains to decide, however, on the basis of Scott's instructions, when silence should be broken. This was not always easy.

The task group now experienced its first communications failure. The signal to launch aircraft was not heard by *Helena*. The catapulting of the planes from *San Francisco* and *Boise* was not seen. Aboard *Helena* the captain's station was the open bridge, a space over the pilothouse giving an almost unobstructed view of sea and sky. The gunnery officer, the assistant gunnery officer, and the communications officer were all here. By 10 P.M. Captain Hoover and his assistants, after almost four hours together, had little left to talk about.

Salt Lake City remained a large shadow six hundred yards ahead, her wake occasionally marked by a faint sparkle. Distant flashes of lightning played on the northwest horizon where the enemy should already have debouched from the Slot. Now he could be only a few miles away if he were here at all. Some kind of a climax to the long, dark approach might be imminent. The circuits from the control stations to the guns had been checked out at regular intervals. Everything was O.K. except the radar at the after main battery controls, which was still out of commission after a week because of missing spare parts.

Helena's plane waited on the catapult, engine idling. Suddenly from *Salt Lake City* there came the insistent buzz of an engine running at full throttle, as though the order had already been given. Then a brilliant ball of white light appeared ahead to starboard. Occasional surfaces of *Salt Lake City*'s superstructure glowed starkly in the intense glare. The light moved to the right like a ball rolling on the surface of the water. At its center was a plane, its tail consumed in fire.

Hoover thought at first that *Salt Lake City*'s plane had been launched prematurely as the result of an accident, but as the moments passed and the silence of the radio continued, he became doubtful. *Helena*'s plane, fueled and armed, was still idling on the catapult. It could not remain there much longer. The planes aboard the U.S. cruisers at the Battle of Savo Island had been fully fueled in keeping with the practice of being ready to fly at all times. When their ships were hit, shrapnel and flying debris turned the gassed-up planes into torches which ignited adjacent parts of the ships.

Scott had been emphatic at the Espiritu Santo conference. Any aircraft on board would be dry and unarmed before entering an engagement. Hoover decided that use of the TBS was warranted. He called Scott, asking permission to launch. The seconds passed, but no answer came.

It was possible that Scott had announced a change of plan and did not intend to have any planes in the air. The message, for one reason or another, might not have reached *Helena*. If *Helena*'s plane were launched now, it might wreck the new plan in trying to carry out the old. The plane itself might be endangered by friends unaware of its identity. And it was too late now to remove fuel, ammunition, and pyrotechnics and keep the plane on board.

Hoover soon gave the order. In the darkness on the fantail the plane's engine stopped. The catapult was trained in, the crane attached. The pilot and observer climbed out as others punctured the light metal float. Then the plane was lifted, swung over the side, and dropped, a casualty of imperfect communications. *Helena*'s TBS receiver was apparently at fault.

The task group continued its northerly course. The two scout

planes aloft had commenced searching. At 10:25, with Cape Esperance abeam, Scott ordered a change of course to starboard to a track
headed direct for Savo Island. It would take the ships much closer to
the Guadalcanal shore. At the same time he made the signal "Dou-
bleheader," his code word for the command to form for battle.

San Francisco turned to the new course when the signal was executed, the other cruisers following single file in her track. The destroyers left their positions in the arrowhead and hurried to their new
ones, three ahead of the cruisers, two astern, so that all now formed a
single column of nine ships. Their order from ahead was *Farenholt,
Duncan, Laffey, San Francisco, Boise, Salt Lake City, Helena, Buchanan,* and *McCalla.*

Disposed along this column was a total of nineteen 8-inch, thirty 6-
inch, and fifty-six 5-inch guns, twenty-five torpedo tubes, and perhaps
six thousand men. If targets showed up on only one side of the
column, eighteen of the 5-inch guns would remain idle. These were
mounted on the opposite sides of the cruisers, and thus would be unable to bear on the enemy.

The purpose of any battle formation is to position ships so they
can bring the maximum number of weapons to bear upon the enemy.
The formation must also allow quick and easy maneuvering to maintain this situation as the enemy maneuvers to improve his own. No
formation is without its disadvantages.

A single column, if not too long, is usually best for bringing the
maximum number of weapons to bear. But the enemy can counter
this by placing himself at right angles directly ahead or astern, crossing the T, and offering full broadsides to batteries whose fire in his
direction is almost completely blocked. Furthermore, the column
does not have the flexibility enjoyed by a formation of separate but
coordinated groups.

However, a column of ships faces less danger of blocking the line
of fire of friendly ships or, in low visibility, of losing touch with each
other or—worse yet—failing to recognize the enemy. In column a
ship can maintain visual contact with the vessel ahead, even on a
dark night. It can keep its proper position simply by following the
leader when signals for changes of course by column movement are
missed.

If spectacular results are less likely in column, so are costly failures caused by a lack of practice in more complex formations. Scott's destroyers were unpracticed in delivering a coordinated torpedo attack, a maneuver which required fine teamwork. The gun was his best weapon. In a simple column it could be used to the best advantage and deficiencies in training could be minimized. Under the circumstances, the choice of formation was sound.

The use of torpedoes by destroyers was not ruled out by the column formation. In his instructions Scott had directed individual destroyers to fire torpedoes at the larger targets as they appeared. U.S. destroyer torpedoes could run at any of three different speeds, the distances they could go being shorter the higher the speed. Because a target could not be expected to hold a steady course and speed indefinitely, a hit was more certain when the torpedo had to run only a short distance at high speed. It was therefore an axiom that targets should be approached to within range of a high-speed shot before firing, if at all possible.

Navy tactical thinking visualized destroyers as a sort of cavalry in fleet engagements, charging in close to deliver torpedo attacks against the enemy's battle line. Although advances in gunnery had long since made this perilous by day, it was still a good maneuver with a practiced body at night. It could be performed by single ships with much less practice.

In view of Scott's preference for the column formation and the advantages it offered, it seems probable that he intended the destroyers to fire torpedoes from column rather than to charge out individually to closer range. His instructions were not specific. There were reasons favoring either method. Had he enjoyed the benefit of hindsight, he might have sharpened his wording.

In column, Task Group 64.2 extended three miles from the bow of *Farenholt* to the stern of *McCalla*. Aboard *San Francisco*, Scott was a little ahead of the middle of the column. He could see neither end.

The southeast breeze, coming directly from Guadalcanal, carried the heavy odor of invisible jungle vegetation. *Farenholt*'s lookouts were sweeping the darkness methodically with their binoculars. Each covered an assigned sector. The gunnery radar, the only one installed, was out of commission.

At 10:45 a profile became visible to starboard, a dim, ragged line separating dark sky from darker earth. Here the track was six miles off the beach and nearly parallel. The beach itself was invisible in the solid black mass of land behind it.

Enemy ships could be lying in close, lost in the same background. Suddenly two blue lights appeared, well forward and to starboard. They looked like dim stars but were almost at beach level. In a few seconds they were gone. They were not reported by *Farenholt*, perhaps on the assumption that they were seen by the flagship.

San Francisco, however, had not seen the lights. On the flag bridge Scott waited with the three young officers who were the commissioned members of his staff. The ship's signal gang stood nearby in a few small knots, talking in low voices, watching, keeping out of the Admiral's way. Officers and men had been waiting for four and a half hours. They had reached their destination, but the faint skyline to starboard was inscrutable.

The first break came at 10:50. A message came in from Lieutenant John A. Thomas, pilot of the *San Francisco* plane: "One large, two small vessels, one six miles from Savo off northern beach Guadalcanal. Will investigate closer."

The message raised several questions. Were all three vessels together? If so, they were being reported as sixteen ("one six") miles from Savo Island. If not, one was six miles from the island. But then where were the others? And where were the other five ships reported earlier that day? If the plane had sighted a cruiser and two destroyers, another cruiser and four more destroyers were still to be found.

If the three vessels were together off the north coast sixteen miles from Savo Island, they were not far from the line separating Japanese and U.S. ground forces, though a bit on the Japanese side. In this visibility the pilot's estimate of distance could well be faulty. Perhaps these were U.S. ships on the U.S. side of the line. If so, Scott should have been informed by Comsopac. But there could have been a slip-up.

Whatever these vessels were, most, if not all, of the quarry were still at large. If the three vessels were hostile, he was between them and their base and could deal with them later. Scott held his course and speed, waiting for further developments.

The present course would put the task group near the portal between Savo Island and Cape Esperance, through which the Japanese had penetrated two months before to win the Battle of Savo Island. Scott's track passed close to the spot where the victors had launched their first torpedoes at the unsuspecting Americans. Scott's plan, as stated in his instructions, was to remain outside the portal until the enemy's location had been established.

He would then strike in whatever way promised the most success. He had never before been in the kind of fight he was looking for tonight, nor had any of his captains. If action came, it could sweep away the pessimism that had been dogging U.S. naval operations in the South Pacific since the Battle of Savo Island—or it could magnify it. The stakes were high.

At 11:05 there was a stir in the flagship when a white light was sighted briefly on one of the mountain tops to starboard. What it meant was anybody's guess. At 11:10 *Farenholt* was at a point nine miles from Savo Island. Scott changed course to the northeast to put the island a safe distance to starboard of the track. At 11:30 Savo was four and a half miles abeam of *Farenholt*. This was as far as Scott intended to patrol in this direction.

Now messages came in from each scout plane. *San Francisco*'s plane reported the location of the three ships seen earlier as being sixteen miles east of Savo Island and one mile off the northern shore of Guadalcanal. This apparently was their location at the time of the earlier report. The *Boise* plane reported that it was landing in the water with engine trouble. This meant that even without opposition from the enemy, only one of four aircraft was still available for scouting. It was discouraging. At 11:33 Scott reversed the course of the task group to continue the patrol.

With the formation in a single column in which there was no grouping of ships for tactical purposes, there were two ways of reversing course. The first was by simple column movement, in which the leader made the turn and the others followed like a string of railroad cars behind a locomotive on a hairpin bend. The second called for a simultaneous turn by all ships, like reversing the slats of a venetian blind, with the first ship becoming the last in column on the new heading, and the last, first.

The second method obviously was much quicker. The time involved in the maneuver was only that required for a single ship to turn around. This simultaneous turn required all ships to come around at the same rate to avoid disorder and the disintegration of the formation. This, in turn, demanded that all ships receive the signal. In contrast, the column movement could be carried out even if some failed to get the word. Perhaps that is why Scott chose the column movement, preferring to take a longer time to turn about rather than risk confusion with the enemy so close.

Farenholt—the lead ship—put her rudder left when the signal for the countermarch was executed. The ship commenced swinging. Half way around the semicircle at the top of the hairpin, she was headed at right angles to the rest of the column. *Duncan* had just reached the turning point. *Farenholt's* Captain Seaward and Commodore Tobin looked back through their binoculars. (As the commanding officer of a ship is always called "captain," whatever his rank, so is a squadron commander called "commodore.") What they saw caused sudden concern. Though *Duncan* and *Laffey* were following in *Farenholt's* track, the entire length of *San Francisco* was directly abeam. She, too, appeared to be swinging left as though executing a simultaneous turn. Either *Farenholt* and the two destroyers following her had misunderstood the signal or *San Francisco* had, or had suffered a casualty to her steering gear.

Tobin ordered Seaward to slow down. He had earlier instructed the two destroyers astern to be alert for unannounced changes of course and speed and to follow the movements of *Farenholt* without signal. He would wait now until he could determine whether the other cruisers were going to follow *San Francisco* and what the destroyers at the other end of the column were doing. If they were seen taking position ahead of the cruisers on the new course, he would take position astern of the cruisers. If they followed in the wake of the cruisers, he would put on speed to reach the head of the column again.

Almost at once *Boise* was seen following *San Francisco*. The shapes of the other two cruisers appeared; they, too, followed in the track of the flagship, which now steadied on the new course. The cruisers, in turn, were followed by *Buchanan* and *McCalla*.

Seaward rang up top speed. The column was still making twenty knots. Judging by what he knew, Tobin thought the enemy would probably be to port if he were encountered in the next few minutes. He therefore directed Seaward to go up the starboard side to keep clear of the line of fire to port.

Tobin's uncertainty had been no fault of his own. There had been a misunderstanding in the flagship. Electronic equipment was not yet plentiful. There was only one TBS on board *San Francisco*. It had to be shared by the ship and the flag. There were outlets for transmitting and receiving on the flag bridge and the bridge, but the gear was so designed that both receiver outlets cut out when either station was used to transmit.

When the Admiral on the flag bridge made a signal on TBS, it could not be heard on the bridge. The same signal had to be sent to the bridge by other means. On her last visit to the West Coast the ship had procured an ordinary interoffice "squawk box" system to provide electronic voice communications between the two stations. Now all signals made by the Admiral on TBS were paralleled on the squawk box to the bridge.

The technique—involving two transmissions—was an expedient that invited errors. Now one occurred.

Somehow, the Admiral's order to reverse course by column movement reached *San Francisco*'s captain as an order to reverse course by simultaneous turn. Neither officer was himself at the squawk box. Somebody else, in relaying the signal, had misinterpreted it.

By her unexpected behavior, *San Francisco* threatened to throw the entire formation into confusion. Scott, surprised himself, could not at first help Tobin. If the error had been made by another ship, it could have been disregarded. The maneuver could have continued without the offender, her place in column kept open until she could regain it. But when the flagship moves contrary to signal, all other captains naturally wonder whether the signal, as they received it, reflects the commander's intentions.

Captain Moran in *Boise,* for example, was caught completely by surprise. Either he had misunderstood the signal, or *San Francisco* had, or she had suffered a steering casualty. Since *San Francisco* reported no steering casualty on TBS, he elected to follow her and set the example for the ships astern. By making this choice, Moran excluded Tobin's three destroyers instead of the flagship from the column. The results of this decision would be seen later.

At 11:42 the muddled countermarch was completed. The new course was 230 degrees, approximately southwest. The column, led now by the task group's flagship, *San Francisco,* was shorter by the three destroyers which had earlier been leading. Scott assumed that Tobin would speed up to regain position ahead and did not call him for confirmation.

The TBS, however, abruptly brought other news. *Helena* reported a radar contact at twelve thousand yards on bearing 285, or six miles westward. The message was receipted. (*Helena*'s receiver was apparently working again for she did not repeat the message.)

Helena's contact was in range of even the 5-inch guns. *San Francisco* aimed her gunnery radar in that direction but could get no echo. Could *Helena* have picked up one of the destroyers left behind in the countermarch? The range, if this were true, seemed excessive. But perhaps it had been misread. If the contact were an enemy, it would more probably have been found to port, the likely direction of any enemy ships.

Two minutes later the TBS croaked again, bringing a report from *Boise.* This report further complicated the picture by describing a contact of five "bogies" at a bearing of sixty-five degrees. In the developing and still unformalized voice radio lingo of the U.S. Navy a bogie was an unidentified aircraft. There was no term as yet for an unidentified surface craft (an indication, perhaps, of the relative importance which had been given to the air and surface uses of radar). Could *Boise* have meant five unidentified surface craft?

When not specified, bearings were understood to be true directions: 90 was east, 180 south, 225 southwest. Relative bearing was the direction determined relative to that in which the ship's bow was pointed. Sixty-five degrees relative was on the starboard side of the ship, sixty-five degrees to the right of the direction in which the ship was aimed at the moment.

In *Boise*'s report the word "relative," which was included, was not clearly heard on the flag bridge. Was she corroborating *Helena*'s contact, as was probable if her bearing was relative? Or was she announcing a completely different one nearly astern and on the other side of the column, if her bearing was true? (The procedure standardized later required that all contacts be reported invariably in true bearings.)

There could be an enemy ship or ships to westward as *Helena*'s contact implied. They could discover the Americans at any instant and open fire. But *Helena*'s contact might also be one or more of Tobin's ships. If *Boise*'s contact was in the direction of sixty-five degrees true, nearly astern, *Boise* was very probably on Tobin. Scott had to weigh the danger of having the enemy beat him to the opening gun against the distinct risk of mistaking friend for foe.

This sort of confusion was exactly what Scott had sought to avoid in using a column formation. Now, not only might the three destroyers be assaulted by the rest of his ships, but the enemy he was looking for, alerted by the guns, would most certainly escape. Even worse, the Japanese might be able to inflict further losses on the American ships in the confusion.

In such a dilemma a commander can only choose a course of action consistent with the probabilities as he sees them. Experience had taught Scott that a couple of radar contacts that are in agreement may make a shaky basis for a crucial decision. Here were two contacts in possible conflict. There was at least enough chance that *Helena* or *Boise* or both were on Tobin to justify the delay needed to ascertain his position. At 11:45 he called Tobin on TBS: "Are you taking station ahead?" The reply came promptly: "Affirmative. Moving up your starboard side."

Before Scott could weigh this, *Helena* was on TBS again with an "Interrogatory Roger" and a request for acknowledgment. She was asking for permission to open fire. The member of the staff who took the message replied "Roger."

This was simply a receipt for the message. An acknowledgment following this would have meant that it had been brought to the Admiral's personal attention. In less than sixty seconds *Helena* asked again, "Interrogatory Roger."

Scott probably heard her both times himself. *San Francisco* had reported no contact. Of all the ships present, only *Helena* and *Boise* had made such a report. The evidence was not conclusive. Scott was determined to avoid the mistake of firing into his own ships. As he was mentally framing a reply, the member of the staff at the TBS responded to *Helena's* second request with another "Roger."

At once the night erupted in explosions! Scott looked aft in astonishment. Bright flashes were leaping from the starboard side of the column in quick succession as though trying to overtake each other, sometimes bursting in twos, threes, and fours together. The pulsating glare served only to intensify the darkness.

Then suddenly a blinding light smote Scott's eyes and a deafening concussion slapped his face and left his ears ringing wildly. *San Francisco* had opened fire! For a moment someone else seemed to be in command of Task Group 64.2.

Chapter Four

11:46

HELENA'S CHART HOUSE, the navigator's work space, was immediately aft of the pilothouse. Part of it had been taken over by the SC and the new SG radars. Since it was one deck lower than the captain's station on the open bridge, the captain's radar information went to him by telephone.

On the night of October 11, 1942, the SG was receiving close attention. The revolving spoke of the big, luminous scope, representing the beam from the revolving antenna overhead, swept around like the hand of a clock. Wherever she was, *Helena* was always positioned at the center of the scope. All other objects appeared in a direction and at a distance from the center corresponding to their location with respect to *Helena*.

At 11:25 the coast of Guadalcanal occupied the outer part of the sector extending between southeast and southwest. Cape Esperance, almost due south, appeared in the scope near the middle of the sector. Savo Island, only six miles away, stretched through fifty degrees of the circular picture to eastward.

The column of U.S. ships was a little line of dots extending through the center in a northeast-southwest direction. Six of the dots were northeast of the center, two southwest. *Helena,* seventh ship in column, was at the exact center.

The radar operator's attention was suddenly caught by a slight twinkle as the spoke swung through a point in the blank northwest expanse of the scope. Such indications often amounted to nothing. But he watched for several revolutions of the spoke. The twinkle appeared at the same point on several of them.

Ensign Gash, the radar officer, looked over the operator's shoulder. Together they watched the scope. The twinkle began to appear with every sweep of the spoke; then it began to persist after the spoke had passed and developed finally into a small, glowing dot which remained in view. Gash notified the open bridge.

The contact was at a point twenty-nine thousand yards away, bearing 315, or fourteen and a half miles northwest. The time was 11:30. By then-existing standards this was remarkably good detection of surface objects, but with the SG it was not uncommon.

With the contact at such a distance *Helena* had time to watch, to be certain that this was not a false indication. The gunnery department's plotting room began "tracking" the contact, plotting the successive positions provided by the SG to establish its path and thus determine its course and speed.

In the darkness of the open bridge each officer reviewed mentally the steps he would take to shift controls, to regain communications if damage disrupted the nervous system centered here. At 11:33 Plot reported a tentative solution: the contact's course was 120 (roughly southeast), speed 35 knots. The forward 5-inch gunnery radar had been coached on and now held the contact, too.

Gash reported that the range was twenty-four thousand yards (there are about two thousand yards in a nautical mile) and that the contact was a group of at least three separate ships.

At that moment, Scott executed his signal to reverse course. With two radars registering, there was little doubt that this was a genuine contact. In addition, the countermarch seemed to indicate that the flagship had the contact, too. Hoover interpreted the maneuver as a move to intercept. He expected another signal from the Admiral at any moment.

San Francisco's error slashed the time needed to bring *Helena* to the new course, but it seemed interminable nevertheless. At 11:35 *Helena*'s forward 6-inch gunnery radar found the contact, now 18,500 yards away. At that moment the column was doubled about the turning point with *San Francisco* and *Boise* on the new course, *Salt Lake City* in the turn, and *Helena* and the two following destroyers still on the opposite heading. *San Francisco* and *Boise* were momentarily between *Helena* and the contact.

From Ensign Gash came word that there were at least five ships in the contact and that they were in a formation looking something like the letter T. At 11:36 *Helena* reached the turning point. The gun directors, guided by their radars, ground slowly around from port to starboard, keeping on the contact as the ship swung in the opposite direction.

When the turn was completed, *Helena*'s guns were trained out and matched up with the directors. Still there was no order from the Admiral. The destroyers astern were not yet on the new course. At the SG the situation of Tobin's destroyers had earlier been noted and reported.

Hoover had no scope before him, but the telephone reports were enough. The Admiral's silence had become deeply disturbing. These five enemy ships, for such this contact certainly was, were close enough to take the formation, still awkwardly disposed, under fire. They continued to close rapidly. "What are we waiting for?" The question rang in the earphones of Lieutenant Commander Rodmon D. Smith, the gunnery officer, coming from Plot, Spot One, and other stations. Smith answered them as best he could.

At 11:42 with *McCalla,* the last ship in the column still in the turn, Hoover reported his contact by TBS, now bearing 285, distant twelve thousand yards. There was a "Roger" but no other response. After two very long minutes he heard *Boise* report. The range was closing rapidly.

"Load all turrets!"

Then he heard Scott's question to Tobin and the reply. The reason for Scott's hesitation was now clear. The Admiral feared that the contact might be his own destroyers. Hoover knew there was no chance that this contact could be Tobin's ships.

The range was dropping past six thousand yards. A report came from some station in the ship: "Ships visible to the naked eye!" (Ensign Gash called excitedly to Lieutenant Commander Charles L. Carpenter, the navigator, "What are we going to do—board them?")

An enemy force was within close range, a range at which it would be difficult to miss. The enemy would see the U.S. force almost immediately if he had not already done so. Hoover knew that Scott would have been shooting long ago if he had had the advantage of an SG. By TBS Hoover asked for permission to open fire, requesting an acknowledgment to emphasize the urgency of his message. (Smith immediately alerted all gunnery stations.) He received a "Roger" at once. When a few seconds passed without the acknowledgment, he repeated his question, this time omitting the request for it.

The body of special words and phrases used as symbols to expedite voice radio transmissions (one of them the word "bogie" used by *Boise*) had developed haphazardly. Some were invented, some borrowed, some used in one ocean and not the other. The use of voice radio was so new that the symbols had not yet been standardized.

Now there was serious confusion with another word—"Roger." Standing for the letter R, "Roger" was the symbol indicating the receipt of a message by voice radio. But, in the code contained in the *General Signal Book,* again standing for the letter R, it meant "commence firing."

Helena's gun crews were waiting tensely. The ammunition trains were full, the guns loaded, the directors locked on. The second "Roger" came back promptly.

Hoover had come recently to *Helena* from command of Destroyer Squadron Two. On his last shore duty he had been in the Bureau of Ordnance. There he had become acquainted with the highly classified experimental work in radar and had first recognized its potential. As a squadron commander he had worked to get maximum advantage from the equipment installed in his ships. This included some of the earliest installations of the SG. When he took command of *Helena* he already knew what the SG could do and he had no doubt about it now. The second "Roger" was all he needed.

"Commence firing!"

"Commence firing!" Smith echoed the Captain. In a split second the firing keys in the two controlling directors were pressed closed. The range to the target of the 6-inch battery at the moment of opening fire was only thirty-six hundred yards. Plot had the target formation approaching at a speed close to thirty knots or one thousand yards per minute.

Aboard *Salt Lake City* the SC radar, as in *Helena,* was in the chart house. The captain's station, however, was on the bridge so that it was convenient for Captain Small to slip in occasionally to speak directly to the radar officer, Lieutenant (jg) Chester M. Lee. Through another failure in communications Scott's order prohibiting use of SC radar had not been received and *Salt Lake City*'s SC was very much in use. Lee was watching it closely with the operator, aware of the disappointing performance of the same equipment, or its personnel, in the Battle of Savo Island.

Just short of the turning point during the countermarch, a pip showed in the grass in the scope. Several readings were taken. Before the ship had completed the turn, Lee was satisfied that he had a contact sixteen thousand yards to the northwest, and so reported. The gunnery radars immediately began searching for it.

Small was not so confident as Lee. Even after *Helena*'s report of her contact at twelve thousand yards he was skeptical. His basis, perhaps, was his own past experience with the SC, the probability that the enemy lay eastward rather than westward and, like Scott, a fear that the contact could be one or more of Tobin's ships.

Like Scott, he was unacquainted with the merits of the SG. He, too, had to act in a manner consistent with the probabilities as he saw them. His action was to refrain from passing the buck, a doubtful radar contact, for the Admiral to resolve. It was his responsibility to resolve it, to believe it himself before reporting it.

A ship did not report a visual sighting until the captain or the officer of the deck had confirmed it. No exception had yet been made to this elementary rule in the case of a radar sighting. Accordingly, *Salt Lake City* kept silent. (The Navy later established a system of reporting contacts which relieved captains and officers of the deck from personally evaluating them.) Small, nevertheless, ordered the batteries alerted and the guns trained out in the direction indicated by the SC.

A little later Lieutenant Commander James T. Brewer, the gunnery officer, commenced to receive reports. The first came from Bland, a man he had appointed to act as his eyes in the dark after he had demonstrated outstanding ability in night vision.

"Those are enemy cruisers," Bland reported, "believe me! I been studyin' the pictures. We got no ships like 'em."

Then came excited reports from *Salt Lake City*'s foretop, the lookouts, and even a battery officer at the starboard 5-inch guns who swore he saw enemy cruisers and demanded the reason for the delay in opening fire. The gunnery radars had now acquired the SC's contact.

Small had stepped into the chart house; he questioned Lee further. Lee was certain. Small left quickly. A few seconds later a sudden jerk rippled the long, green curtains shielding the door to the bridge. The discharge of *Salt Lake City's* ten 8-inch and four 5-inch guns roared outside.

Aboard *Boise* the contact was not made by the SG radar until after the ship had completed the countermarch. But the picture was conclusive at once. There was no possibility that these five dots on the screen well out to starboard could be Tobin's ships. They, too, were in plain view and nowhere near. Three of the five dots appeared to be in column with the other two disposed on either side and a little ahead of the column leader, forming a pattern like the letter T. The gunnery radars were quickly coached on, the guns alerted and trained out.

Like *Helena, Boise* assumed there was some relationship between her contact and the countermarch. Scott must be turning to meet the enemy. Anxiety quickly mounted when the flagship's silence continued. When *Helena's* contact report elicited no more than a "Roger," *Boise* made hers. When *Helena* opened fire, *Boise* followed immediately.

Aboard *San Francisco* the SC radar was shut down in accordance with the Admiral's order. The gunnery radars had had no contact up to the time *Helena* and *Boise* had reported theirs. Finally, at 11:44, the after gunnery radar found something to starboard. The discovery was too new to be accepted at once. Radar operators had a tendency to be overeager.

At 11:45 what appeared to be a destroyer came into view on the same side. It was too faint in the gloom to be identified. Captain McMorris heard *Helena's* request to open fire. Nevertheless, knowing Tobin's ships were somewhere to starboard, he was in doubt.

When the firing commenced astern he may have thought he had missed a signal. In any event, the after gunnery radar continued to hold its contact. By its position and movement it became quickly apparent that the contact was not Tobin coming up the starboard side. McMorris opened fire on this target without further delay.

Four cruisers opening fire in face of the commander's obvious reluctance may seem like poor discipline for a first-class navy. Scott had instructed his captains to open fire without order when the enemy was located. This authority did not extend to targets which were clearly in doubt in his own mind. But the best discipline does not require blind obedience. At those rare times when the subordinate can be sure, it demands the action that his commander would desire were he in possession of the same information.

This kind of discipline places the burden of decision upon the subordinate. The burden lies in the need to be certain that one has all the facts and that they fully justify the decision to take action contrary to the immediate intentions of the commander. This was what governed Hoover's action. The other captains, already sharing his misgivings, quickly followed his example.

Such behavior was not unknown in the tradition of first-class navies. Horatio Nelson of the Royal Navy broke formation without permission to cut off the retreating foe at the Battle of Cape Saint Vincent. He thereby enabled his commander to win a sweeping victory.

Hoover was later awarded the Navy Cross for his conduct at Cape Esperance. The award was tacit recognition of his disciplined initiative in opening fire, though it was not specifically cited.

In destroyers it was customary for the executive officer, the second in command, to remain at the after conning station during battle. In the ships of Squadron Twelve this station was located one level above the main deck just aft of the 1.1-inch gun mount and forward of 5-inch Mount Number Three.

The purpose of the exec's presence there was to have the next most experienced officer ready to take control of the ship in case the captain became incapacitated. The ship's capabilities would be severely reduced were the bridge to be destroyed at the same time. The only equipment at after conn was a compass and some telephone connections to other important stations.

The view forward was obstructed by the stacks and the bridge structure but it was possible here to exercise limited control of the ship. With the crew at battle stations the exec might move about before an engagement to ascertain that all was ready. During actual shooting he had little to do but wait here, watch the show, try to keep aware of what was happening (sometimes difficult), and trust that the misfortune required to give him a more active role would not happen.

Except for a few hours of sleep, any time spent at after conn was the only time that the executive officer was not busy. He usually performed the additional duties of navigator. Even then, he did not cease to be the ship's principal coordinator, highly sensitive to the quality of the food, the cleanliness of living spaces, the kind of leadership displayed by the officers, the state of training, and many other matters, all of which he and the captain had to deal with on a daily basis.

Lieutenant Commander Alcorn G. Beckmann, executive officer of *Farenholt,* was at after conn with a couple of telephone talkers when the countermarch commenced. He, too, saw *San Francisco* turning, noticed the sudden hush which came over the topside as *Farenholt's* fire room blowers slowed. For some reason *Farenholt* had reduced speed, seemed to be dawdling. *San Francisco's* entire fore and aft silhouette became slowly visible in the field of his binoculars, then contracted again as she continued to turn. She turned more sharply than *Farenholt* and when both ships had reached the new course the latter was somewhat to starboard as well as astern of the other. *Farenholt* continued to dawdle. The shadows of *Boise, Salt Lake City,* and *Helena* followed silently in the path of the flagship like vessels in tow.

At last *Buchanan* and *McCalla* could be seen coming through the dark in the wake of the cruisers. Then the sound of the blowers rose like a wail and a muffled rumble issued from *Farenholt's* stacks. One of them emitted a heavy puff of smoke hardly visible against the black sky. Slowly a breeze came up from ahead. The bow wave took shape, became a white wing extending out from the side, sweeping up water from the darkness ahead and discarding it as quickly in the darkness astern. A subdued vibration set in, decks, bulkheads, and fittings humming with the rapid whirling of the propellers.

Beckmann had to plant his elbows on the rail to keep his binoculars steady at his eyes. He was puzzled by the maneuver. The ship was running at top speed, apparently to regain position at the head of the column. She made steady progress and by 11:42 had drawn abreast of *Boise*. *McCalla* was just completing the countermarch. All ships except Tobin's were again in a long, straight file. *Farenholt's* track was about nine hundred yards to starboard.

Tobin, on the bridge, could observe that he would be back in proper position in ten more minutes. The prospect was encouraging. Then came *Helena's* contact report. Tobin's situation had been awkward. Now, if this contact was good, the situation was dangerous. He decided to clear the line of fire to starboard by slowing, letting the column draw ahead, and taking position astern. Moving forward to the head of the column would take far too long. It would take even longer if Scott should increase speed.

At Tobin's order, Seaward slowed *Farenholt* again. Then *Boise's* contact report was heard. Tobin was about to turn around to get clear faster when Scott asked by TBS: "Are you taking station ahead?"

The question seemed to indicate that that was what was expected and desired. It was not apparent that Scott's main concern was to determine whether Tobin's ships were the reported contacts. Scott had intended that the three destroyers lead the column in battle. He seemed to be assuring himself that they were returning to that position. Tobin answered, "Affirmative. Moving up your starboard side."

At after conn Beckmann had heard the blowers slow again, had felt the vibration subside and wondered why. Soon speed was resumed. He was unaware of *Helena's* and *Boise's* reports. Suddenly a cataclysm for which he was completely unprepared erupted to port. The gunfire sprang from the dark, a vision of something incandescent, shuddering under the explosive blows of a hundred hammers on an Olympian anvil. The U.S. cruisers were shooting toward *Farenholt*, over and around her, at something beyond!

Aboard *Duncan*, Lieutenant Commander Louis J. Bryan, executive officer, had been on the bridge with Captain Taylor when Scott executed the signal to reverse course. It was easy to see when *Farenholt*, five hundred yards ahead, started swinging.

Her silhouette began to change shape. The black, symmetrical mass, something like the spire of a church, began spreading out irregularly to port as the outline of the bow came into sight on that side. At the same time her wake started to boil, making a clearly visible spot at the right-hand side of the base of the changing silhouette.

There was quiet excitement. *Duncan*'s gunnery radar had just reported a contact to westward. Taylor was not yet ready to accept it as genuine. If genuine, it was almost certainly hostile. If hostile, it was in position to attack the U.S. column at a critical time.

Taylor and Bryan discussed the possibilities. *Duncan,* following *Farenholt*'s lead, had not swung very far when *San Francisco*'s maneuver caught Taylor's and Bryan's attention. Then the distance to *Farenholt* commenced to close rapidly. Taylor slowed to avoid overrunning her.

Radar reported the contact again. It was closer. The flagship's movement could not be explained by the signal she had sent, but it might have some connection with *Duncan*'s contact. This ought to be clarified soon.

Duncan loitered behind *Farenholt* in the turn. The radar still held the contact, which continued to get closer. Taylor had few doubts left. Then, before reaching the new course, *Farenholt* appeared to steady on a heading in the direction of the contact. Did she have it? Was Commodore Tobin about to act? He had previously directed *Duncan* and *Laffey* to follow *Farenholt* without signal.

The contact was coming within gun and torpedo range and the U.S. column was doubled on itself. Quick action was necessary and the destroyers with Tobin were best situated to take it. From the appearance of *Farenholt,* action had already commenced. Taylor rang for thirty knots and alerted all stations. (He did not know that *Farenholt*'s radar was out of commission.)

The ship picked up speed quickly, and just as quickly a mistake became evident. Taylor was astonished to see that *Farenholt* was again, or still, turning slowly left, still idling at low speed. As *Duncan* swept past (unseen, as it turned out), the radar reported again. The contact was still there and still closing. The danger to the column was growing acute.

To slow down, turn around, and regain her former position would take the little remaining time *Duncan* might otherwise use to prevent a possible disaster. Taylor (captain of the Navy football team in 1924) decided to attack alone. It was a decision in the best destroyer tradition. Unfortunately, no report was made to the Admiral.

Duncan continued to accelerate. She lifted a little and dropped abruptly as she crested unseen swells so gentle they were not noticed at lower speeds. Behind the screen at the chart desk in the pilothouse the quartermaster illuminated his notebook with a very dim, red flashlight and wrote: "@ 2341 CS to 30kts, CC to 255T." The radar continued to hold the contact, which tended to drift left. Taylor adjusted course left to intercept.

The radar reports quickened as the range dropped. At five thousand yards someone cried out. He had the contact in sight, thirty degrees on the starboard bow! A formless smudge had appeared there and began to take shape.

At first it was a long, low, indefinite shadow. Then a superstructure began to emerge from the dull background. Incongruous words issued suddenly from the TBS: "Are you taking station ahead?" "Affirmative. Coming up your starboard side." (*Helena* and *Boise* seem not to have been heard earlier.) The outlines became sharper, bow and stern clear. The contact was moving from right to left, her entire length visible in profile.

The heavily raked stacks, the forward much larger, the distinctive curve of the stem, and the sloping appearance of the deck near the stern were unmistakable. This was a Japanese cruiser! The vision had the quality of a dream. The vessel was moving at good speed but she looked peculiarly serene. Her turrets were trained in and her decks appeared to be uninhabited. Two bursts of light suddenly flashed near her bridge. They were followed at once by a cascade of crackling, reverberating thunderclaps. The clock in the pilothouse read 11:46.

Laffey, following *Duncan* in the turn, had been mystified both by *San Francisco*'s unexpected movement and *Duncan*'s unexplained departure. Having no radar contact, she remained astern of *Farenholt,* following her changes of speed. *Helena*'s report at 11:42 seemed to bear a relation to *Duncan*'s disappearance. The exchange between Tobin and Scott, followed by *Helena*'s first request to open fire, was extremely disquieting. Captain Hank observed that he was abreast of *Helena.* When firing suddenly commenced, he acted at once.

Buchanan and *McCalla,* bringing up the rear, were also confused by *San Francisco*'s actions. *Buchanan* might have turned at once and led *McCalla* to a position ahead of the cruisers on the new course. This was not what the signal called for, however, and Captain Wilson of *Buchanan* had no idea what Tobin was doing. He decided to remain where he was rather than risk compounding the confusion.

In succession the two destroyers reached the turning point and came to the new course. They heard the reports of *Helena* and *Boise,* the exchange between Scott and Tobin, and *Helena*'s requests. Their radars, their lookouts, were still searching when the cruisers ahead opened up.

Thus, when firing commenced at 11:46, the cruisers, followed by *Buchanan* and *McCalla,* were in column on course 230 (nearly southwest) making twenty knots. *Farenholt,* on the same course on a track nine hundred yards to starboard, was making thirty knots or more, *Laffey* following. *Farenholt* was abreast of *Boise; Laffey* was abreast of *Helena. Duncan,* unknown to Tobin, to Scott, and to most if not all other ships except *Laffey,* was completely separated from the formation. *Farenholt* and *Laffey* were between the formation and the target, and *Duncan* was close to the target itself.

Chapter Five

THE FIRST MINUTE

AT 2:00 P.M., ten hours before the first flashes of gunfire broke the darkness at Cape Esperance, a second group of Japanese ships had gotten under way at the anchorage at Shortland Island. This group consisted of three cruisers and two destroyers.

The cruisers were the sister ships *Aoba, Furutaka,* and *Kinugasa,* each named for a mountain lying in the vicinity of a naval base in Japan. The destroyers were *Fubuki,* "Snowstorm," and *Hatsuyuki,* "First Snowfall of the Year."

The three larger ships constituted Cruiser Division Six, and were of the *Kako* Class. *Kako,* the prototype and fourth ship of the Sixth Division, had been sunk by a U.S. submarine while returning to base after the Battle of Savo Island. The other three had also taken part in that crushing victory over the Americans two months before. Today, with the two destroyers, they sailed as the Support Group under Rear Admiral Aritomo Goto, Sixth Division Commander. If the group's designation meant anything, its mission was to support the Reinforcement Group. It would do this principally by shelling the Guadalcanal airfield that night, grounding aircraft that might otherwise attack the Reinforcement Group on its return trip.

The movements of the two groups were coordinated at the Rabaul headquarters of Eighth Fleet, to which each group belonged. Both were carrying out subordinate parts of a broad plan which had been in effect since early in the month.

According to the plan, troops, equipment, and supplies were being ferried into Guadalcanal almost nightly, in a build-up which would culminate in a ground offensive intended to recapture the island completely. Daylight bombing and nighttime naval shelling of the U.S. airfield would accelerate until, by the start of the offensive in the middle of the month, the field would be knocked out, at least temporarily. Then it would be possible to bring down a large, slow convoy of merchant-type ships with the massive back-up needed by the ground forces to press the newly launched offensive to a quick, successful conclusion.

The Reinforcemennt and Support groups knew each other's timetable. The Reinforcement Group's schedule was quite different because of its lower speed and the extra time it needed to unload heavy equipment. The faster Support Group could operate under more conventional timing. It started a 30-knot run-in from the two-hundred-mile mark at sunset. It needed no air cover. Although it would close the distance to the Reinforcement Group on the way, the latter would still reach Guadalcanal two hours earlier. This sort of scheduling may indicate the lack of opposition expected by Eighth Fleet after darkness set in. The Support Group would return by the same route, the Central Track, directly through the Slot, by which both groups had approached. The Reinforcement Group would return via the Southern Track, skirting south of the Russells, New Georgia, and Rendova.

Running on schedule, the Support Group reached the two-hundred-mile mark at sunset, then increased speed to thirty knots. No enemy aircraft had been sighted. In fact, the hard-pressed field at Guadalcanal, already watching the approach of six destroyers and two "cruisers," had not sent out a late reconnaissance to the upper end of the Slot. Furthermore Henderson received no warning from the Coast Watchers, who had missed this movement, and never discovered that the Tokyo Express was running two sections this trip.

Goto's cruisers were in a column headed by *Aoba,* the flagship, followed by *Furutaka* and *Kinugasa* in that order. The two destroyers were at a distance on either side of the column, twenty degrees forward of *Aoba*'s beam, making a pattern like the letter T with the crosspiece forward, *Hatsuyuki* to port, *Fubuki* to starboard.

Almost at once the ships ran into a series of heavy rain squalls. Visibility at times dropped almost to zero. If such weather were present at Guadalcanal, it would be unwise to try to shell the airfield. Navigation would be hazardous and it would be difficult, in any event, to find the target because Japanese ships had no radar.

Each of the cruisers mounted six 8-inch guns and a secondary battery of four 5-inch, two per side. The destroyers each carried six 5-inch guns. Both types of ship carried smaller automatic guns and torpedoes.

Torpedoes received particular attention in Japanese naval planning. Under the terms of the Washington Conference agreement of the early 1920s, Japan limited herself to three-fifths of the strength in battleships granted to the United States and Great Britain. When the Imperial Navy sought means of overcoming this disadvantage, it turned to that great leveler, low visibility. The idea was to depend on smaller ships, on which there was no numerical limitation, to redress the balance of naval power by stealth.

Darkness would cover the approach of the light forces, blinding the long reach of the heavy-caliber gun. Then, the torpedo could be launched unseen and unheard. It would hit by surprise.

Research, new construction, and training were all conducted with this tactic in mind. Telescopes, binoculars, and range finders of unequaled power were developed to insure greater range of vision in the dark than any adversary might enjoy. Torpedo size and performance were improved.

At the outbreak of World War Two the Japanese had a torpedo with roughly the same speed and range characteristics as the American torpedo, but which carried half again as much explosive. More important, it was more reliable than anything the Americans had. The Japanese frequently used "live" torpedoes in practice. As a result, they detected and eliminated defects in the firing mechanism. In contrast, reluctance to expend torpendoes in practice because of the expense was reflected in unreliable U.S. torpedo performance long after the war had started.

Furthermore, Japanese torpedo crews were drilled intensively to develop speed in loading and reloading and in making firing adjustments in the dark. Destroyer captains, torpedo officers, and officers of the deck were so well acquainted with the standardized procedures by which a squadron launched a coordinated torpedo attack that it had become a routine maneuver requiring few signals.

The Imperial Navy was proud of this hard-earned accomplishment and rightly conscious of its superiority in this kind of fighting. The Battle of Savo Island served only to confirm this opinion.

This was one reason that Admiral Goto might have felt confident. Another was that reconnaissance aircraft had reported no enemy warships in the vicinity of Guadalcanal during the day. Also, U.S. ships usually left Guadalcanal at nightfall. And by 10:30 P.M. the Reinforcement Group should have arrived at its destination. Since no word had been received from it by that time, there was added reason to believe that the only opposition to the bombardment might be the weather.

The Support Group pressed through squalls and violent lightning and thunder. At 10:30 Savo Island was forty-five miles ahead. At this point, Goto sent a message to the Japanese base at Guadalcanal asking the state of the weather. He received a reply that it was fair. Reassured, he steamed on. He did not suspect that the lightning flashing about the Support Group was being observed by nine U.S. warships.

Nisshin and two destroyers of the Reinforcement Group had anchored at a position along the Guadalcanal north shore about sixteen miles from Savo Island. Henderson Field lay only ten miles away. Feared by day, this hornets' nest was ridiculously harmless at night. Unloading was in progress when, at 10:45, the sound of an aircraft was heard. It was certain the plane was hostile. Gun crews stood alert. Unloading into landing craft sent out from the beach continued. Lights were not being used. The plane passed overhead and continued on its way. Hope faded, though, when the sound returned. The sound swelled and declined several times.

The plane made no effort to attack. This might have suggested that its purpose was reconnaissance. In any event, it was too early to take alarm. In the absence of further developments unloading continued. No report was made to the approaching Support Group.

The latter was steaming at thirty knots through repeated squalls, blinding flashes of lightning, and blasts of thunder. By 11:30 it was near its objective. Admiral Goto would soon have to decide whether to go through the passage between Savo Island and Cape Esperance blind, trusting to dead reckoning and hoping for more visibility inside, or instead to remain outside waiting for the weather to improve. No word had been received from Guadalcanal to indicate that the visibility there had deteriorated.

The question was resolved when, at 11:35, the group suddenly emerged from the long belt of storms which had filled the Slot and sighted the seventeen-hundred-foot peak of Savo Island a few miles ahead. The Admiral ordered speed reduced to twenty-six knots to keep his schedule.

Next the cruiser *Aoba* sighted three shapes, like ships, about five miles ahead and a little to port. This, at least, is what is stated in the report later submitted by the captain of *Aoba,* acting as commander of Cruiser Division Six. Such a sighting, had it occurred, would have caused immediate, serious concern. The shapes would soon have been identified as ships. Although they could have belonged to the Reinforcement Group—out there for some unknown reason—they could also have been hostile.

The report fails to indicate whether the alarm was passed to the other ships. Apparently, the Support Group continued to rush ahead on the same course, almost directly toward the unknown ships which were already within gun and torpedo range.

"The commencement of battle action was ordered," says the report. But before it could commence a wall of explosions erupted like a submarine volcano. At this instant the clock on *Aoba*'s bridge read 11:46. The report contains nothing to indicate that battle stations were yet manned and ready.

The Japanese had run blindly into the American column stretched across their bows. Had the suspicious shapes been sighted at five miles, as stated, there would have been at least six minutes before 11:46 in which to deploy. Something could have been done. Given Scott's uncertainties at this time, Goto should have been the one to open the battle.

The failure of the Japanese lookouts, usually so efficient, is difficult to explain. One or more ships of the Support Group were visually sighted by *Helena* at six thousand yards, by *Duncan* at five thousand. In contrast, at the Battle of Savo Island U.S. ships were sighted with the superior Japanese optical equipment from the cruiser *Tenryu* at fourteen thousand yards.

Poor visibility due to background or a local atmospheric condition could have been a factor, but the main culprit probably was a state of mind. Goto had not sent his crews to battle stations. Therefore, it was obvious at all levels of his command that he did not expect to meet the enemy. It is hard work to concentrate continuously on a dark horizon. Vigilance can be exhausting. When superiors act as though their efforts are unnecessary, lookouts can be expected to relax. And probably they did.

The blame falls—as it should—on Goto's shoulders. But there were contributing factors. He could logically have expected *Nisshin* to warn him of signs of possible opposition. By eleven o'clock, thanks to the persistent surveillance of *San Francisco*'s plane, *Nisshin* should have realized that some kind of enemy activity was afoot. Unfortunately for Goto, *Nisshin* did not warn him.

Perhaps the thinking at Japanese Eighth Fleet Headquarters encouraged a complacent attitude. If the purpose of the Support Group was to support the Reinforcement Group, why should it have been scheduled to reach Guadalcanal two hours behind the group it was meant to protect? Eighth Fleet apparently considered the need for protection against surface craft remote.

When the American cruisers began firing at 11:46 P.M., an astonished Beckmann at *Farenholt*'s after conn rushed to the starboard side to see what they were shooting at. With the sky breaking apart behind him, he looked out to see dozens of low-flying meteors crossing ahead, astern, and overhead, streaking in almost level flight like streams of hot sparks. They were converging at points out in the dark near eye level. The points were marked by occasional flashes which seemed to have been produced by the collision of the meteors with something unseen. Suddenly four star shells burst about half way between horizon and zenith. Evenly spaced from left to right, the stars lighted up a wide expanse of ocean. Their glow was small at first, but it quickly grew large and bright. It spread in all directions and extended down to light the surface. Then Beckmann saw the targets.

Three ships appeared under the slowly descending stars. They seemed motionless, transfixed in the moment of discovery. They were amazingly close—only one or two miles away, disposed roughly abreast and separated from each other by a considerable interval. The center ship was almost directly abeam and pointing at *Farenholt*. The other two lay parallel to her.

Beckmann thought he saw a column of other ships behind each of

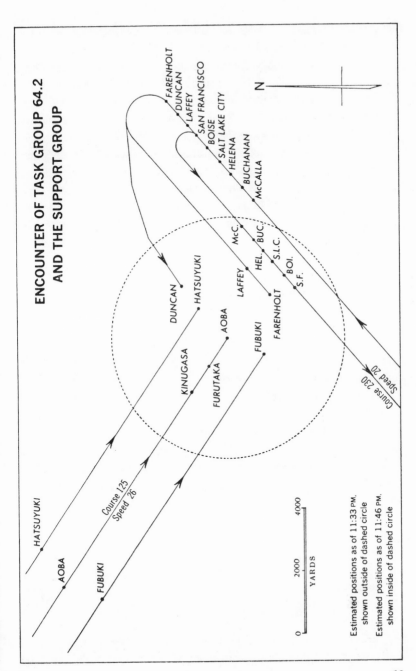

ENCOUNTER OF TASK GROUP 64.2
AND THE SUPPORT GROUP

N

HATSUYUKI
AOBA
FUBUKI

Course 125
Speed 26

FARENHOLT
DUNCAN
LAFFEY
SAN FRANCISCO
BOISE
SALT LAKE CITY
HELENA
BUCHANAN
McCALLA

DUNCAN
HATSUYUKI
KINUGASA
AOBA
FURUTAKA
FUBUKI
FARENHOLT

McC.
BUC.
HEL.
S.L.C.
LAFFEY
BOI.
S.F.

Course 230
Speed 20

0   2000   4000
YARDS

Estimated positions as of 11:33 P.M.
shown outside of dashed circle
Estimated positions as of 11:46 P.M.
shown inside of dashed circle

the three leaders. He could not tell how many ships were in the columns, nor could he identify the leaders. But they seemed to be cruisers. They had not yet returned fire. Caught in the first few seconds of the star shells' bright, unnatural light, the ships had the unconcerned appearance of rocks jutting up from the ocean.

Suddenly *Farenholt's* 5-inch Gun Number Three, hardly twenty feet aft, opened up, temporarily deafening and blinding Beckmann. The gun was in an enclosed mount and gave no warning. Beckmann rammed some cotton into his ears while the spots swimming in his eyes subsided. He soon saw that Number Three was firing star shell and that the other 5-inch guns, shooting in salvo, had taken the left of the three ships under fire. (They had opened at a range of eighteen hundred yards on what was believed to be a cruiser twenty-five degrees forward of the beam.)

Aboard *Laffey* the blast of *Helena's* aroused batteries was reverberating in the pilothouse. A wall of fiery bursts thrown up by the other cruisers extended ahead to port. Hank acted without delay.

"All engines, back emergency full!"

In *Laffey's* after engine room the turbines, reduction gear, feed pumps, everything, were running at high speed. The combined noise was so loud that one had to shout to be heard above it. Suddenly there was a sharp jangling of a gong. The engine order telegraph—a white pointer which indicated the required speed on a large dial—ran up and down several times, finally stopping on "Astern Full." The throttleman grabbed a spoke of a large, brass wheel labeled "Ahead" which was mounted vertically on the control board and started to spin it clockwise.

A chief petty officer who had been standing behind him reached for a knob on the engine order telegraph. He twisted it back and forth several times, then gripped a similar wheel, not quite so large, next to the throttleman's. A sleepy-looking youth who had been standing to one side wearing a telephone headset suddenly came to life, shouting, " 'Mergency! Give 'er all ya got!"

The chief looked up at the gauges, then turned his wheel a few revolutions counterclockwise, while the throttleman continued to crank desperately. This permitted steam to enter the backing turbine before the supply to the ahead turbine was shut off. A high-pitched whine came from the blades of the backing turbine now acting as a brake.

The chief turned momentarily, saw a man standing expectantly at a couple of nearby valve wheels mounted at the upper ends of reach rods extending from beneath a grating. The chief made a quick gesture. The new man responded by turning one valve wheel and then the other. At this, the roar of the main circulator swelled and joined the whirling clatter.

Next, the chief opened the backing throttle a few more turns. Then, as the throttleman finished, the chief spun the wheel rapidly the rest of the way. The needle on the gauge showing the propeller shaft speed dropped quickly down to zero as the full volume of steam poured into the backing turbine. The legend "Astern" flipped into view in a little window and the needle started up again without a pause. Without a word the chief stepped back and the throttleman moved in front of the backing wheel.

As the propeller picked up speed in the reverse direction, *Laffey* started to bump and shimmy as if she were grounding. The chief and the throttleman paid no attention. They were watching the needle of the gauge marked "Main Steam." It was dropping slowly, indicating that the backing turbine was devouring steam faster than the boilers were making it. If the pressure were dragged down too far, the fuel pumps and other auxiliaries which used the same steam would fail, extinguishing the boilers. This had to be avoided at all costs.

A few seconds passed and the needle still dropped. The chief, taking his eyes off the gauge for a moment, nudged the throttleman, and gestured, describing a clockwise circle in the air. Slowly, almost reluctantly, the throttleman gave the backing wheel a few clockwise turns and the pressure stopped dropping.

Looking down into the water from the wing of the bridge, Hank could see that he had knocked off much of *Laffey*'s headway.

"Starboard engine ahead full! Left full rudder!" (This left the port engine, the one in the after engine room, still backing.)

On the gauge board in the after engine room a pointer on a dial marked "Rudder Angle Indicator" swung all the way left. The man at the circulator controls reached for a rail as the ship heeled to starboard. Overhead piping began to vibrate severely. The men at the board kept their eyes on the gauges, shifting weight to keep balance.

A minute later the engine order telegraph clanged again and stopped on "Ahead Full." Again both the chief and the throttleman took a wheel, too busy to observe that the rudder was swinging back amidships.

When the chief stepped back, having said never a word, the ship had returned to an even keel and the heavy vibration had ceased. The propeller shaft was turning ahead. The throttleman made a small adjustment, lightly striking the rim of the ahead wheel with the heel of his palm. He reached for a clip board hanging close by. A form marked "Bell Sheet" was attached. He took the pencil dangling by a piece of string, paused, and looked at the clock. It read 11:47.

"Whatcha doin' up there?" asked the telephone talker, speaking loudly and a little anxiously into his instrument. *Laffey* had come about and was speeding for a new position astern of *McCalla* at the rear of the column.

When Taylor saw the bursts of light around the bridge of the Japanese cruiser and heard the guns, he immediately put *Duncan*'s rudder right. He, too, started to clear the line of fire. The cruiser crossed his bow rapidly as *Duncan* started swinging. The opportunity to attack was delayed.

Taylor was on the port wing, still watching the target, and preparing to turn back before losing it, when Bryan called him urgently to the other side. Broad on the starboard bow was another shape. Taylor saw at once that she was another cruiser. She looked like the first and seemed to be following her. Her guns, too, were trained in.

Still swinging right, Taylor decided to take her under fire and gave the preparatory orders. He would steady on the opposite course and, still forward of her beam, launch torpedoes, then attack with gunfire.

But things happened too fast. Taylor's attention was called back to port where he saw still another ship, headed nearly the same way as *Duncan*. She, too, appeared to be in a right turn, a turn toward *Duncan*. She was hard to distinguish, but Taylor thought she might be *Laffey*. She was in such a position that, if he steadied on the course he had chosen and she continued to turn, she might run into him.

There was nothing to do but keep on turning. *Duncan* turned past her firing course. The other ship disappeared in the darkness while the intended target, still on the same course and apparently unaware of *Duncan*, was drawing off on the port quarter.

Taylor had missed a perfect set-up for a torpedo shot, but there was still a chance. He called for full left rudder. The helmsman spun the wheel and in a few seconds the ship was turning sharply in pursuit of the cruiser, which was still clearly visible. *Duncan* continued to turn until she had brought the other ship on her starboard bow. This was not the ideal position—the target was headed away—but it would have to do. The range was still short. At Taylor's order a torpedo leaped from the tube and hit the water with a solid slap. A few seconds later the 5-inch battery opened fire.

Up to this moment the engineers in *Buchanan* and *McCalla*, unlike their counterparts in the other three destroyers, had enjoyed a quiet evening. Since the ships had formed in a column at 10:25 there had been no deviation from their 20-knot speed. The keyed-up feeling which had gripped the engineers when the hatches were dogged down over their heads at 6:15 had dissipated. Now it returned with a cold thrill at the warning just received from the bridge.

Neither ship had been able to find the contacts reported by *Helena* and *Boise*. The men on each bridge had heard *Helena*'s requests to open fire and were not surprised when the cruisers suddenly commenced.

For the first few seconds the dazzling discharges distracted them from their search for the target. Streams of tracer bullets flew in shallow arcs. Each cruiser's tracers had a distinctive color. To Lieutenant Commander Floyd Myhre, *McCalla*'s executive officer, the scene was a rapid series of violent rainbows arching out through the dark from the U.S. column. Then a spread of stars burst to starboard, opening like great, glowing flowers.

Lieutenant Commander William G. Cooper, *McCalla*'s skipper, now saw in silhouette what appeared to be a friendly destroyer two thousand yards off and forward of the starboard beam. Just to its left, at twice that distance, he saw the profiles of a cruiser and a destroyer, which he recognized as enemy. From another position topside Lieutenant (jg) George T. Weems, *McCalla*'s damage control officer, saw two ships "large and ghostly, but with their guns trained fore and aft." Cooper picked one of the two enemy ships as his target.

McCalla's engineers stood below tensely, watching their machinery with painful concentration. Since 10:25 the myriad spinning parts had joined in a deep, monotonous hum of unvarying pitch. Suddenly there was a quick tremor as though the ship had received a light, side-wise thrust. At the same time, a sharp, tinny clap burst from the forced ventilation outlets. Each spat out a handful of dust. Over the background of customary noise one heard for a moment a subdued, sonorous roar. Eyes met briefly, returned to the machinery. The humming continued like even, powerful snoring, heedless of the one, solitary salvo.

In the engineering spaces aboard *Buchanan* they were still waiting.

At the time she opened fire, *Helena*'s main battery was aimed at what was thought to be the right hand of the contacts to starboard. It was thirty-six hundred yards away and already ten degrees abaft the beam. With the target group on an estimated course of 120 degrees, this ship would pass astern of the entire U.S. formation if it continued. The secondary battery's target was a few degrees to the left.

Nine of *Helena*'s 6-inch guns were ranged in three turrets along the first hundred feet of deck immediately forward of the bridge. Nine muzzles, pointed at a target already abaft the beam when firing commenced, swung slowly closer to the bridge as firing continued and the target drew further aft.

The main battery had opened in continuous fire. The guns, kept continuously on the target by remote control, fired individually as quickly as they were loaded, and loading arrangements, highly mechanized, were fast. On the open bridge, the eye and ear were almost overpowered. There was no let up in the blinding, pounding flashes, the hot, jarring blasts from the muzzles.

Salt Lake City was the oldest ship in the U.S. column; she had been commissioned in December, 1929. And she showed her age in many ways. Among other things, she lacked the high degree of water-tight compartmentation built into later ships. Her eight boilers were distributed four apiece in each of two fire rooms. In contrast *Helena*'s eight boilers were distributed two to each of four fire rooms. Whereas *Salt Lake City*'s telephone network connecting the battle stations was powered by electricity originating in the ship's generators, *Helena*'s electricity for the same system came from the mechanical force of the voice striking the diaphragm in the mouthpiece. *Helena*'s system worked without dependence on an outside source of power. *Salt Lake City*'s guns were aimed by their individual crews in response to signals received electrically on dials; the more modern *Helena*'s guns could be aimed without any human intervention at all. Age figured elsewhere in *Salt Lake City*'s armament. With older and slower systems of bringing up and loading ammunition, the best rate of fire her main battery could attain was considerably slower than *Helena*'s and she normally fired in salvos.

At Captain Small's order ten shells burst from the ten steel tubes of *Salt Lake City*'s main battery. Clearing the muzzle with a massive, fiery report, each 265-lb. projectile headed for the target at a speed in excess of twenty-six hundred feet per second. Ten orange balls sailed into the dark. They were like a flock of luminous birds speeding directly away, rising a little then dropping a little, seeming all the time to draw closer together.

Brewer, watching through his binoculars, saw several faint white splashes where the orange balls disappeared. Six spotters were watching for them. Two spotters were in the masts, two in the high turrets, and two on the main deck at either end of the ship. Their job was to estimate the distance between splashes and target.

Spot One in the foremast was receiving the reports of the others by telephone and determining the correction to be applied to the aim. Fire had been opened with radar readings alone on a target forty degrees forward of the starboard beam, and four thousand yards out. The four starboard 5-inch guns, however, had opened with the main battery using star shell. Just after the second salvo was fired, the first stars opened. Spread out in silhouette to starboard *Salt Lake City*'s eager gunners saw several ships—all apparently enemy and all unbelievably close.

Boise had opened with the first sound of firing astern. Her main battery was on a target almost abeam at forty-five hundred yards, her secondary covered another a little to the left at only 3550 yards. With a few exceptions, *Boise* and *Helena* were similar ships. Their main batteries were alike. Like *Helena*'s, *Boise*'s guns were shooting in continuous fire.

Moran's problem was like Hoover's. With nine of his fifteen 6-inch guns exploding in his face, he still had to control his ship. Half blinded by the continuous flashes, he could no longer see the outlines of *San Francisco*. Only the flash of her guns assured him that he was still astern of her.

San Francisco's first salvos were directed by radar at something twenty degrees forward of the starboard beam, some forty-six hundred yards out. There had been no time to advise Scott of the contact before opening fire. McMorris was convinced that his target was hostile, and since the ships astern had already revealed the presence of the task group, no delay was warranted.

To Scott, on the flag bridge, the circumstances which had led the four cruisers to open fire were not nearly so clear. If he had known more about the SG, he would have placed more reliance on the reports of *Helena* and *Boise*. He did not know that the other two cruisers and one destroyer had also acquired radar contacts in the same general position moving in the same manner, and that these could not have been Tobin's ships.

Added to this, other information Scott could have had was missing to an unfortunate extent. *Helena* had not reported her contact before the countermarch commenced, when there could have been no question about the location of Tobin's destroyers. *Boise*'s report had not been received clearly. Otherwise it would have corroborated *Helena*'s contact. Scott knew the enemy could be encountered to starboard but, on the basis of available information, expected to meet him to port. All he knew for sure, as a result of his TBS exchange with Tobin, was that the latter was overhauling the column on a parallel track at an unspecified distance to starboard. The moment was urgent.

"Cease firing! Cease firing!"

Scott's order was passed promptly over TBS at 11:47, one minute after the cruisers had fired their opening shots.

Chapter Six

MIDPOINT

SCOTT HAD CROSSED THE T and did not know it! Goto had unwittingly led his ships into a dead end. But this situation could easily have been reversed. This seems apparent even though the relative positions of the ships of the two sides at 11:46 can only be approximated from the record. Also, the two groups were so close and moving so fast that a small inaccuracy can have a disproportionate effect upon any conclusion.

When the firing started, the U.S. column lay across the Japanese line of advance about two miles ahead of *Aoba,* the lead enemy cruiser. This positioning was a direct result of *San Francisco*'s misunderstanding of the countermarch signal. If *San Francisco* had not turned at once, but followed in the track of the destroyers ahead of her, as she should have, *Farenholt* would have remained at the head of the column. On the new course of 230, the head of the column should have been about a mile behind where it actually was when *San Francisco* became the leader by mistake. At twenty knots it would then have taken another three minutes to cover this mile and bring the column to the same position it arrived at with *San Francisco* leading.

In the same three minutes the Japanese, at twenty-six knots, would have advanced another twenty-six hundred yards. *Aoba* would then have been only fourteen hundred yards from the U.S. column. In less than two more minutes the column would have been breached somewhere near the middle.

Tobin's destroyers, of course, would have been safe in formation. Knowing this, Scott would presumably have opened fire long before. The example shows, however, that the countermarch, correctly executed, was timed to bring about a collision.

71

In the actual situation timing was so critical that, if permitted to continue undisturbed, the Japanese cruisers would have passed astern of the U.S. column. In the absence of initiative such as Hoover's, Goto—not Scott—would have crossed the T. If the Americans had followed the same track with the same movements five minutes later, or if the Japanese had come five minutes earlier, Goto would have been in position to cross ahead.

Far from appreciating these possibilities, Scott was trying to keep his own ships from firing at what he still thought were friendly destroyers. The cup of his frustrations, already filled with aircraft failures and a botched maneuver, was running over. Although the order to cease firing was repeated over TBS several times, there was no immediate decline in the volume of fire. Even Scott's own flagship continued firing. In the uproar, the order did not reach Captain Mc-Morris.

San Francisco's first target was burning. Another ship, a little to the right, was also burning. Now a third was seen in the light of stars fired from another U.S. ship. She was approaching from the beam. McMorris ordered both batteries to take her under fire. The 5-inch scored one or more hits almost immediately and the glow of a small fire showed briefly between her stacks.

Suddenly Scott's voice rang out on the bridge between salvos. He had come up the ladder from the flag bridge. To the astonishment of all present, he heatedly delivered an order to cease firing. Then he disappeared as rapidly as he had come. The guns fell silent. McMorris was too concerned with the closing target to be flabbergasted.

When he returned to the flag bridge Scott noticed that the volume of fire astern of *San Francisco* had dropped somewhat. He had the cease-fire order repeated periodically.

In the meantime, Scott tried to ascertain the fate of Tobin's ships. His first question on TBS revealed his fears. It was not "Where are you?" but "How are you?" Tobin answered "O.K." and added, "We are going up ahead on your starboard side." Scott was not satisfied. "Were we shooting at Twelve?" "I do not know who you were shooting at," was the reply.

Farenholt, which Scott may have seen by this time, had been drawing close to the line between *San Francisco* and her recent target. Mc-Morris, realizing that this may have added to the Admiral's concern, sent assurances that *San Francisco* had been firing at targets well beyond *Farenholt*. Scott, still not convinced, ordered all destroyers to flash their recognition lights. These were a vertical display of three lights mounted over the bridge. The color of each light could be varied so that a number of combinations were available. A different combination was used each night and served as a visual means of distinguishing friend from foe. On this night the combination was green over green over white.

Aboard *San Francisco,* Captain McMorris, Lieutenant Commander William W. Wilbourne, the gunnery officer, and all the gunners continued to watch the ship they had been firing at last. She still approached. *San Francisco*'s guns, still loaded, were kept aimed at her.

When she reached a position about fourteen hundred yards abeam she came right to a parallel course. She did not make the green over green over white signal, but flashed a dim light; its beam was directed down into the water. It seemed to be a signal of some kind but was unintelligible to those aboard *San Francisco*. Then a vertical display, a white light over a red light, flashed on and off. These could have been the foretruck light and the port side light.

Suddenly Spot Two was calling Wilbourne frantically to announce that this was a Jap! "For God's sake, shoot!" If he were right, *San Francisco* should be struck by torpedoes in the next moment. Wilbourne, having no order to commence firing, directed a searchlight on the stranger. A destroyer glowed at the far end of the beam. Her superstructure was unfamiliar and the two white bands which boldly encircled her forward stack caused every man who watched to catch his breath. She was already turning sharply away.

"Commence firing!"

The end of McMorris' shouted order was drowned in the roar of the guns. The target seemed to increase speed. The first two 8-inch salvos straddled her, some shells falling beyond, some short. The third salvo scored at least one hit. An explosion erupted at the base of the after stack. The fourth salvo caused a huge explosion, and the destroyer seemed to part in the middle. Her bow disappeared at once and her after half, wildly unstable, rose to a near-vertical position, propellers and rudder visible in the searchlight beam. Then it sank. She had not fired a shot in return.

The first glimpse of the ship transfixed in *San Francisco*'s searchlight beam corrected Scott's misconceptions. The time was 11:51. Now he passed the order at once to commence firing, after having tried for four minutes to stop it. Later in his action report, he said: "It took some time to stop our fire. In fact, it never did completely stop." Now the volume swelled instantly.

With the sinking of the destroyer, *San Francisco* searched for another target, preferably one still undamaged. The lull enabled Scott to make a quick but uninterrupted survey. He saw several shapes briefly. But they were obscured in the flicker of fires, smoke, and gloom, and were being fired at by several ships in the column astern. They appeared to be heading westward and drawing away. To pursue them, he signaled a change of course at 11:54 to a little north of west. He then sent off an urgent radio dispatch to Comsopac and the Commanding General, Guadalcanal: "Engaging heavy cruisers."

San Francisco had no sooner reached the new heading when Lieutenant Commander Bruce McCandless, the communications officer and the officer of the deck at this time, pointed something out to McMorris. It was a dim white light ahead and to starboard. Through binoculars one could see that it was a ship drawing closer and moving in a direction which would take her across *San Francisco*'s bow.

The batteries were alerted. As the ship continued to approach, she was identified as another destroyer. A dim red light soon appeared under the white, which was seen to be mounted on the foremast. It was exactly like the display shown by the destroyer *San Francisco* had just sunk. Similarly, another white light suddenly appeared under the red, blinking a series of dots and dashes.

McMorris delayed no longer. The target was so far forward that only the two forward turrets could bear on it. The first 8-inch salvo straddled the destroyer but made no hits. The 5-inch splashes were all "overs." The second 8-inch salvo, fired dead ahead just as the destroyer was crossing the bow, was also a no-hit straddle. At this instant a report from the signal bridge reached McMorris. "It's the *Laffey* calling the *Farenholt!*" McMorris ordered both batteries to cease firing.

McCandless had seen the dots and dashes but had recognized no meaning. He continued to watch through his binoculars as McMorris returned to the starboard wing of the bridge. The destroyer, now on the port bow, was heading aft. Suddenly he saw some small flashes of light on her deck amidships. He knew they might be of no significance but in these close quarters he took them to be caused by the firing of torpedo impulse charges.

At once he ordered full left rudder and called the captain. If torpedoes had been fired, he hoped to turn short and avoid them, at the same time taking a course to ram the other ship. McMorris ran to the port side to find his ship swinging rapidly in the direction of a collision. He had accepted the report from the signal bridge as accurate, and he had not seen the flashes observed by McCandless.

"Right full rudder!" He did not even wait for an explanation from McCandless.

The two ships passed on opposite courses at what seemed like no more than a hundred yards. By the time McCandless could describe what he had seen, the stranger had disappeared in the darkness on the unengaged side of the U.S. column. *San Francisco* resumed the westward course.

Boise's spotters had a better view than their skipper, Captain Moran. Higher above the guns, they were able to protect their eyes from flash blindness. They identified the main battery target as a cruiser and directed a stream of 6-inch shells at her at a rate of one a second. After firing for three minutes, they believed they saw the target go down by the bow, her screws still turning, her turrets still trained in.

The secondary battery target, a little to the left, was never seen by eye. Not only the target but the splashes, too, were watched in the radar scope. An early spot caused the splashes to straddle the target, and this one, too, was soon apparently sunk. The target pip disappeared from the scope with the splash pips still showing. Firing was stopped. Reports from other stations indicated the victim was a destroyer which was seen breaking in two before sinking.

Both batteries were now shifted to a third ship in sight in the same vicinity. For a full minute *Boise* drenched her with shells. Then an explosion enveloped her and she, too, disappeared from view and from the radar scopes. At least three ships seemed to be burning in the area to starboard, so badly aflame that they appeared to be out of action. The gunners searched for something more dangerous.

At 11:53 a cruiser with characteristic Japanese lines was sighted and both batteries opened fire. At the starboard 5-inch guns, the men were slowed by flash blindness. They had to walk more carefully to avoid stumbling while carrying ammunition. They had to load more deliberately to prevent accidents.

Then came the first hint that this engagement might not continue to be completely one-sided. White columns of water sprang up on both sides of *Boise*. Two or three splashes were only fifty feet to starboard. They cascaded down like Niagara, soaking the 5-inch guns' crews on the same side and adding slippery decks to their troubles.

Next there was a sharp explosion quite different from the report of a 5-inch gun. The superstructure bulkhead in the vicinity of this battery had been struck. One of the guns lost power and communications and the aiming mechanism of another was jammed. Three of the men were stung by small metal fragments. Flames glimmered through holes in the bulkhead. The main battery and the other two 5-inch guns continued their fire. Again a fire lighted their target. It burned very brightly, enveloping the enemy ship in smoke. Her shooting ceased. At 11:57 several violent explosions were seen in her direction. *Boise* ceased firing for lack of a target.

Throughout all this, Moran kept *Boise* astern of *San Francisco* as best he could. Blinded by his own guns, he apparently did not see her turn to port to ram the strange destroyer but found her when firing was suspended at 11:57 still forward of the beam.

He steered to resume station astern and noted that *San Francisco* had settled on a westerly heading. He had not heard the change of course signaled over TBS. Neither had he heard the order to cease firing at 11:47 nor that to commence at 11:51. The TBS had been completely drowned out amid the violent sounds of gunfire.

Salt Lake City's guns were not yet warm when the order to cease firing came at 11:47. The cruisers immediately ahead and astern continued as though the order had not been given. The two burning ships to starboard would have been reassuring had there not been others there. Every second of delay was an invitation to disaster. Captain Small had to suppress a strong impulse to resume firing.

Salt Lake City's original target had been lost in the darkness when the last star was quenched but the lookouts found another approach-

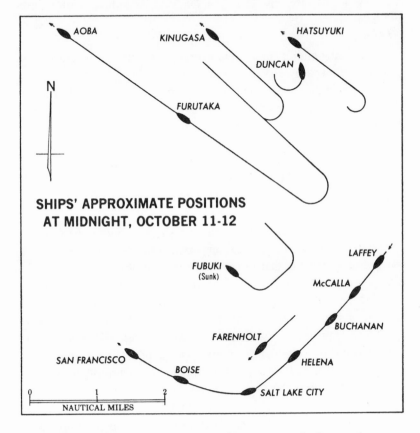

**SHIPS' APPROXIMATE POSITIONS
AT MIDNIGHT, OCTOBER 11-12**

AOBA

KINUGASA

HATSUYUKI

DUNCAN

N

FURUTAKA

LAFFEY

FUBUKI
(Sunk)

McCALLA

BUCHANAN

FARENHOLT

SAN FRANCISCO

BOISE

HELENA

SALT LAKE CITY

0   1   2

NAUTICAL MILES

ing from the beam. A gunnery radar was coached on, the guns quickly matched up. The target remained dark. At the order to commence firing at 11:51 the gunners released a salvo at a range of five thousand yards. The starboard 5-inch battery again fired star shell.

In the turrets there was a deafening hiss of compressed air as breach blocks swung open. "Bore clear!"

There was a clatter of loading trays and the sharp, musical ring of shells driven firmly into their seats by the power rammers. Powder bags were shoved in quickly behind the shells, trays pulled back, breach blocks swung closed.

"Ready Two!"

Lights came on at the control station as each turret indicated its readiness to fire. By this time Spot One's "Down three double oh!" had been applied.

"Shoot!"

The warning buzzer sounded in every control station, at every gun, and was followed by absolute silence.

Then the firing pointer at the director pressed the buzzer key again with one index finger, the firing key with the other. Both were mounted like triggers. Salvo two burst from the guns. From the foretop the target was seen for only an instant against a spread of stars which had just started to open. She was thought to be a cruiser. When the smoke cleared, she was gone.

The gunners searched for another target. At 11:55, they saw a quick twinkle of light, and realized it was a ship shooting at them. A plume of water sprang into the air just short of *Salt Lake City*. It rained down with a curious rattling more like hail than the fall of water. But everything that rained down was not water: a man in one of the control stations was killed by a piece of flying shrapnel.

The Marine top sergeant who controlled the automatic weapons battery, and who happened at the moment to be close to Brewer, could not suppress an observation. "Commander, *this* is the business!" Bland, hearing him, countered with another impression. "This ain't *no* place for anyone who wants to enjoy his old age!"

For some reason the near miss was not followed up. Before its source could be located, another target was found near the beam, some seven thousand yards out. Hits were scored on the third salvo and on the three following.

Again star shell was used. The target did not seem to be a cruiser or destroyer and might have been some kind of auxiliary. Several men thought they saw her roll over and nose steeply down as she sank, her propellers still turning.

There was little time, however, to exchange impressions. Another

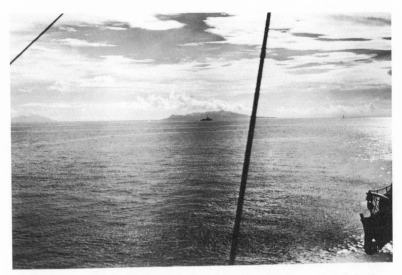

Looking west from Ironbottom Sound with Cape Esperance at left, Savo Island in center. U.S. Navy

A patrol of Marines starts its trek on a mission at sunset on Guadalcanal. U.S. Navy

Heavy cruiser *San Francisco* at Pearl Harbor. Undamaged at Cape Esperance, she received many hits in the night battle of November 13, 1942, off Guadalcanal. Her main battery mounted nine 8-inch guns in three turrets. National Archives

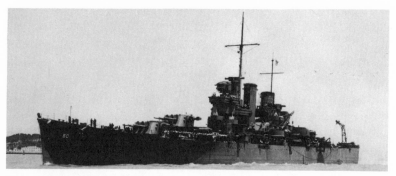

Light cruiser *Helena*. Undamaged at Cape Esperance, she was sunk nine months later in another night battle farther up the Slot. Ship's main battery consisted of fifteen 6-inch guns. U.S. Navy

Destroyer *Farenholt*. She was moderately damaged at Cape Esperance. National Archives

Destroyer *Duncan,* sunk at Cape Esperance. U.S. Navy

Destroyer *Laffey,* which was sunk in the night battle of November 13, 1942. About a month before the Battle of Cape Esperance, she rescued survivors from carrier *Wasp;* some of them may be on board here. U.S. Navy

Destroyer *McCalla,* showing radar antenna on top of 5-inch director, 5-inch gun mount to the right, and torpedo tube mount to the left, aft of the forward stack. This area in *Duncan* was badly hit during the battle. U.S. Naval Institute Photo Collection

Heavy cruiser *Salt Lake City* was moderately damaged at Cape Esperance. Her main battery of ten 8-inch guns was distributed among four turrets. U.S. Navy

Japanese *Kako* Class cruisers, the type that fought in the Battle of Cape Esperance, were 595 feet long and had main batteries of six 8-inch guns in three turrets. Twelve torpedo tubes carried 23-inch torpedoes. U.S. Navy

Rear Admiral Norman Scott, Commander Task Group 64.2 at the Battle of Cape Esperance. Scott was killed a month later in action off Guadalcanal. National Archives

Captain Gilbert C. Hoover, commanding USS *Helena*. National Archives

Lieutenant Commander Edmund B. Taylor, commanding USS *Duncan,* in a picture taken after he had been promoted to the rank of captain. National Archives

Marine Dauntless dive bombers took off from Henderson Field for battle missions. Note bomb under belly, gunner in rear seat. Pilot attacked by placing plane in deep power dive at target, releasing bomb at the bottom of the dive. U.S. Navy

Henderson Field featured open air repair shop facilities, temporary housing arrangements, and a pagoda for Marine and Navy fliers. U.S. Marine Corps

An Army Air Force B-17, similar to the plane that first sighted the Japanese Reinforcement Group, attacks an enemy position in the Solomons. U.S. Navy

A Curtis SOC, like that which burned and crashed on launching from *Salt Lake City,* takes off. U.S. Navy

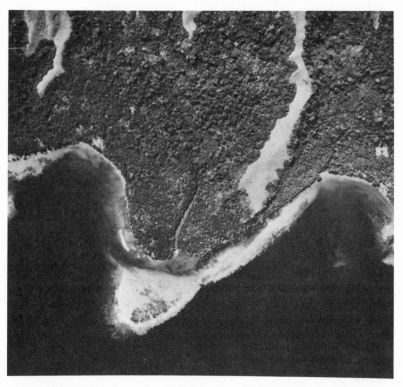

The northwest tip of Guadalcanal near Cape Esperance as it appeared on December 29, 1942, while still occupied by the Japanese. Tate and Morgan struggled past this shore in their raft. The white areas offshore are coral reefs. Coconut plantations can be seen along the beach. National Archives

A Grumman F4F Wildcat of a U.S. Marine fighter squadron taking off from Henderson Field to repulse an attack by Japanese bombers. U.S. Marine Corps

ship was seen by the lookouts approaching at high speed from the starboard quarter. The searchlight beam revealed a destroyer. The main battery fired only one salvo. The range was only fifteen hundred yards. When the smoke cleared, there was no more destroyer. The searchlight was doused.

Helena's main battery—the first guns to break the silence—fired without pause for about two minutes. As in *Boise,* Scott's order to cease firing went unheard. The target, still tracked by radar, seemed to be holding its original course and speed. Then, suddenly, it vanished from both the gunnery and SG radars. Fire was checked.

Lieutenant Warren C. Boles, Spot One, saw nothing in the area where the shells had last fallen except a dense cloud of smoke and an occasional glow of flame. There were three burning ships well to the left. A long burst was fired into the cloud and Boles and others looked hard for an indication of results. There was nothing to be seen.

The main battery next shifted to the target under the fire of the 5-inch battery. The new target was the right hand of the three burning ships. After another roll of continuous fire it disappeared. Some observers later described it as a *Kako* Class cruiser and expressed certainty that it had rolled over and sunk.

Buchanan was about to commence firing when Scott's "cease fire" was heard at 11:47. When the "commence" order came four minutes later, and with it the illumination provided by *Salt Lake City,* Captain Wilson saw three destroyers on the starboard hand forward of the beam and then, directly abeam, a larger ship on a parallel course. He believed he saw in her long, rangy lines a cruiser of the *Kako* Class.

He opened fire on the cruiser at only thirty-five hundred yards. Other ships were also firing at her. She was hit repeatedly and flames broke out at several points along her length. Then Wilson launched a spread of five torpedoes.

At 11:56 two large columns of water, taller than shell splashes, rose almost simultaneously at points along the cruiser's side. She slowed at once, dropped aft, started to settle, and then appeared to break in two and sink. *Buchanan*'s guns were shifted to one of the destroyers on the starboard bow. She soon caught fire and seemed to be sinking.

Another ship now appeared abaft the beam. In the garish, uncertain light she looked like some kind of transport or, perhaps, a small, older cruiser. Since she seemed to be undamaged, Wilson took her under fire. About a hundred rounds later, she was burning and fleeing toward the northwest.

McCalla had fired just one salvo when "cease firing" was heard at 11:47. But she managed to hold her target through the pause and started firing at once when the "commence firing" order came. The other enemy ship which had been close by was still there. The two—a cruiser and a destroyer—seemed to be steaming in column on a course parallel to the U.S. column. The cruiser was in the lead. When one of the two targets disappeared in smoke, fire was shifted to the other. In the uncertain, wavering light of the American illuminating stars, Captain Cooper identified the cruiser as one of the *Kako* Class.

Watching from deck farther aft, Lieutenant (jg) Weems twice thought he saw this sequence of events:

At first, complete darkness. Then, a stream of tracers from one or more U.S. ships. Next, a series of flashes marking the impact of shells on an unseen target. Then, a glow of stars suddenly revealing the outlines of the target ship. Next, fires and explosions. Finally, the target folding in two, then sinking.

By 11:58 both of *McCalla*'s targets were burning fiercely. In another two minutes both had disappeared.

Laffey had completed the long S turn she had started under the blast of *Helena*'s first guns. When she commenced firing at 11:51 she was in column astern of *McCalla* and sharing her targets.

Farenholt, trying to clear the line of fire by pulling ahead, was not so fortunate. At after conn Lieutenant Commander Beckmann stared in fascination through his binoculars. He saw the flashes of projectiles striking one of the enemy ships. The ship turned slowly to its right, until finally it settled nearly on a parallel course with its full broadside revealed.

Beckmann recognized the shape—the distinctive curve of the stem, the two slanting stacks, the forward very much thicker. He had seen those lines before, but only in pictures. In the fluctuating, shadowy illumination, punctuated by the flash of *Farenholt*'s guns, she seemed very close. Her turrets, miraculously, were still trained in.

Now, she was hit aft. Blinks of light that started to walk forward along her length marked the impact of projectiles delivered by a U.S. ship in a long burst of continuous fire. They moved relentlessly until they reached a point under the bridge. Then abruptly the scene was blotted out by smoke.

Overhead Beckmann saw tracers in strings like illuminated streams of water. He saw lights flying in bunches. Sometimes there were several bunches in the air at once. When a U.S. cruiser turned on a searchlight briefly, he was uncomfortably aware that *Farenholt* was being silhouetted. He saw *Farenholt*'s recognition lights flash on and off once. The globe of one light appeared to be shattered, causing it to show white instead of green, another did not burn at all.

A little later he felt a sharp, burning sensation in his cheek and reached up to pull out a splinter of steel shaped like a small nail. His clothing was strangely damp and he discovered that the deck was wet. He had just turned around to look to port when he was completely drenched by a solid wall of water dashed aboard from that side. He and the others at after conn dropped flat. They were reminded by the vibration of the deck plates against their stomachs that the ship was still running at high speed. Three or more geysers to port spewed over them. *Farenholt,* unrecognized, was being fired on by a friendly ship!

Back on his feet again, Beckmann could see no immediate sign of damage but the vibration had fallen off and he could tell the ship had slowed down. *Farenholt*'s guns were silent though the battle continued elsewhere. The telephone talkers could get no immediate information as to what had happened. Then the door in the housing of Number Three Gun Mount opened and a junior officer jumped out to ask indignantly what the engineers were doing about the "power failure."

Unknown to Beckmann, the ship had been hit. First, a shell had exploded in the rigging near the top of the foremast. Fragments had cascaded down, hitting several men. One of the fragments hit the middle tube of the torpedo tube mount which was swinging in from port, past the forward stack, to take aim to starboard. The fragment pierced the tube and the air flask of the torpedo within. The resulting release of high-pressure air kicked the torpedo part way out of the tube and into the sheet-metal apron surrounding the base of the stack. Here it caught, jamming the tube mount. The torpedo's motion had caused the starting lever to trip and the engine made a complete run, high and dry, inside the tube.

At 11:55 a second shell had struck. It penetrated near the water line, causing the flooding of several compartments. Electric cables were cut; centralized control of the guns was lost except for telephone communications with those forward. Hunks of the exploding shell pierced the forward fire room bulkhead, causing several high-pressure steam leaks in that space. It became necessary to secure Number One Boiler. The crew remained to keep Number Two on the line.

"We'll steam her into Tokyo!" was the reply given when they were ordered to abandon the space if it became too hot. Three minutes later a third shell crashed directly into the fire room, riddling machinery and causing more steam to roar out through broken connections. The crew escaped without injury and just ahead of a fatal scalding.

By now, the ship had lost half her motive power. She was flooding, and her battery could no longer be centrally controlled. Scott's fears had not been altogether groundless. The shell holes were both on the port side, apparently received with the series of shorts which had soaked the men at after conn.

The action aboard *Duncan* had reached a peak. One of her torpedoes was drilling through the water in pursuit of an enemy cruiser she now had under fire. Nobody on the bridge saw or heard the forward stack go. A shell struck it near the base. The hit knocked it down and killed most of the men of the forward repair party stationed in the vicinity.

Meanwhile, the target shook with a heavy explosion. *Duncan*'s torpedo had apparently run true. Her guns now were shifted to another ship, probably a destroyer, that was sighted at close range to starboard. *Duncan* got off two salvos and then was struck a massive blow. Two shells came at the same time. One plowed into the ammunition handling room under Gun Number Two, just forward of the bridge. It exploded, killing or wounding the men there, and starting an intense fire. The second smashed into the superstructure over the pilothouse, destroying gunnery and torpedo control apparatus, and wounding several men, including the torpedo officer, Ensign R. A. Fowler.

The forward engine room received a report from the forward fire room. The forward boilers had been disabled by the hit that had knocked over the stack. The crew there was directed to secure the boilers and evacuate. A second report soon came. The boilers were secured but the crew would remain to put out a small fire and would leave when "everything is straightened out."

When the forward stack went over, it threatened to fall on the torpedo tube mount and the torpedo crew jumped for safety. The stack missed and Chief Torpedoman D. H. Boyd went back just as the torpedo control station was knocked out. He could still see the cruiser target. The tube mount was still pointing in its general direction. The phones were dead. Without further delay he made a rough estimate, aimed the tubes, and fired another torpedo.

Guns One, Three, and Four fired a few more rounds in local control but soon lost sight of their destroyer target. From the bridge the cruiser could still be seen. She was under fire from other ships. Shell splashes surrounded her. In their midst another column of water rose, close aboard, higher than the others. Another torpedo appeared to have hit. Suddenly she seemed to crumble in the middle and roll over. Then she disappeared.

There was no time for cheering. Taylor called for left rudder to get clear. It seemed altogether possible that *Duncan* had been hit by friends, and he ordered the recognition lights turned on. He had already felt *Duncan*'s speed dropping. Added to this, he could no longer communicate with his guns. A severe fire raged directly forward of the bridge and an undetermined number of the crew were dead or injured.

The knockout blow came as the ship started swinging. A tremendous jolt and a deafening concussion shook the bridge. The man who had been standing next to Taylor was killed. So were three others. The chart house was a burning wreck, a pyre for the five men inside. The steering gear and engine order telegraph were useless. The recognition lights were extinguished. There was no electric power on any equipment. There was no communication with any part of the ship by telephone, and it was soon apparent that it was not even possible to send a messenger.

The fire in the handling room blocked escape forward. Another fire, even larger, was rising immediately aft from the depths of the forward fire room. Smoke and steam blowing up from a large hole over that space filled the pilothouse. The heat of the fire forward made it impossible to open the air ports for ventilation.

Taylor could receive no report of conditions beyond the walls of fire forward and aft. He could make no determination of what should be done to save the ship. Nor could he issue any orders beyond the bridge. Vast damage had effectively relieved him of command. Looking over the side, he could see that *Duncan* was still moving at considerable speed and circling to the left. The rudder was left, still where it had been at the moment power had failed.

The Japanese had experienced calamity at the very outset. The lightninglike flashes of gunfire extending in a line across the bow had barely commenced, the first thunderous crack of artillery had just sounded when shells crashed into the cruiser *Aoba*. One or more exploded on the bridge and at the Admiral's station. Nearly every man present was knocked down—some dead, some wounded, some only stunned. The captain, one of the few unharmed, assessed the situation.

His ship was still careening headlong into destruction, her speed still unimpaired. Several illuminating stars were glowing pitilessly in the sky astern, revealing *Aoba* with brutal clarity. (The Japanese thought they were flares dropped by aircraft.) Shell splashes were leaping from the water ahead and to the sides. Fires had broken out and the ship was hit forward again. Communications with the gun control stations were cut. But it was still possible to get orders to the engineers and to steer from the bridge.

How much the captain could see of the other force at that moment, its disposition and heading, is unknown. He put the rudder right without order from the Admiral and called for smoke.

Aoba swung. When she reached a westerly heading the captain started to zigzag, hoping to throw off the murderous fire. The engineers responded to his orders rapidly. Both stacks were spouting floods of thick, woolly, impenetrable smoke even before the turn was completed. The maneuver worked. Behind the smoke, *Aoba*'s men who were still able struggled to restore communications, extinguish fires, clear wreckage, and move the dead and wounded.

Furutaka, following *Aoba,* was equally surprised. Her skipper's first startled impulse was to turn left but he reversed rudder to follow *Aoba* when she was seen turning right. But a shell hit a ready torpedo tube and started a severe blaze. As a result of this, and while *Aoba* was concealed in smoke, *Furutaka* took a heavy concentration of fire.

Kinugasa, the third cruiser in the column, also turned when firing started. She may have started to follow *Furutaka,* but when the other reversed her rudder *Kinugasa* continued to turn left and became separated from the other two ships. *Hatsuyuki,* the left destroyer, also turned left and followed *Kinugasa.* There is no record that any Japanese ship saw *Duncan* during these confused moments. What *Fubuki* did is uncertain except that a few minutes after 11:46 a burning ship—which the Japanese thought was *Fubuki*—was sighted from *Aoba.* A little later there were several heavy explosions and she was no longer seen. (This might have been *Duncan.*)

The movements of the Japanese ships had been taken individually; no signal had come from the flagship. *Aoba*'s captain, completely preoccupied with the problems of his own ship, was soon informed that Admiral Goto had been badly wounded. The command of the Support Group now fell upon him.

There could be no worse time to take over. In the awful confusion of the moment, the Support Group had all but disintegrated. It was now impossible to command the movements of even two ships. It was a case of every ship for herself. Each would have to get clear of this murderous position individually, escaping, if possible, to a distance where coordination could be re-established. Even then it would be difficult to command from *Aoba*. Most of her communications equipment was down.

Aoba soon turned northwest to the most direct route of escape. *Furutaka* followed, but heavy damage, including, perhaps, one or more torpedo hits, had reduced her speed. She fell behind. Nevertheless, she was able to bring at least some of her main battery to bear on what appeared to be the third ship in the enemy column, a heavy cruiser. She inflicted what she thought was fatal punishment.

Kinugasa, once on a northwest course, was able to train out her guns quite unmolested. At 11:52 she commenced firing at what seemed to be a cruiser and was confident of having administered severe damage before losing sight of her target. So far, neither she nor *Hatsuyuki* seemed to have been observed by the U.S. ships.

By the time *San Francisco* had returned to course after the lunge at the strange destroyer, the U.S. formation had fallen into very ragged shape. *Boise* was off on the starboard quarter. Some ships had dropped behind, extending the length of a long formation. The ships toward the rear had not yet reached the point at which *San Francisco* had changed course westward at 11:54. The column, insofar as it was revealed by the flashes of gunfire, was a long, curving tail with some secondary waves.

The composition and disposition of the enemy were still obscure. But whatever his strength and whatever his intentions, Task Group 64.2 would be more effective if more concentrated. The enemy seemed to be trying to escape. Scott saw no sign now that he was even shooting back. Accordingly, he ordered "Cease firing" and directed his ships to close up, flashing recognition lights occasionally to expedite the process. The course was still westward, the speed still twenty knots, the time midnight.

Chapter Seven

DISENGAGEMENT

ON THIS MIDNIGHT AT CAPE ESPERANCE the world of every observer had shrunk to a stretch of water covered with darkness and smoke and the glint of fire. It was hard to believe that anything else existed.

Ten minutes earlier Scott had undergone the ordeal of a commander losing control of his command. Now, although he was still uncertain about much of the situation, he could smell victory. He did not know the strength and disposition of the Japanese force. Nor did he know what damage, beyond the loss of one destroyer, he had inflicted upon it.

Most of the firing had died down and Scott and his captains were each trying to piece together a coherent picture from the impressions which had reached them directly or through the reports of their subordinates. Visual observation had been restricted to a narrow field most of the time. One tended to look down the tunnel through the dark made by one's own tracers. One did not always see that other ships shared the same target. One saw other ships firing, but was not always certain who they were or what they were firing at.

Illumination had not lighted the enemy completely or continuously and was not equally effective for all observers. The SG radars in *Helena* and *Boise* made it possible in theory to distinguish friendly and enemy ships at all times. But the enemy formation had dissolved, while the American formation had loosened up. Both groups had become so nearly intermingled that the scope was strewn with a handful of pips in no discernible pattern. The operators, inexperienced by later standards, soon lost the identity of most of the pips.

Moreover, *Boise*'s SG went out of commission with a blown fuse after the battle started, and remained out for five minutes. When it was restored the most expert operator could not have identified all pips in the changed picture. Despite radar, this battle was still a game of blindman's buff. The Americans knew only that the enemy was trying to break away and that most of the U.S. force was still steaming and ready to shoot.

Boise was still shooting. She had failed again to hear the order to cease firing. Just before it was transmitted she had engaged a ship revealed by a brief outbreak of flames. With radar providing the range, she fired for about two minutes. The target finally disappeared from the scope and from view and she stopped for lack of another.

Seeing the flash of *San Francisco's* recognition lights, Captain Moran brought *Boise* more nearly astern of her. For two or three more minutes the guns of the task group were almost completely silent. This ended abruptly when brisk firing was resumed by a ship astern. *Boise* still could find no target.

Meanwhile, the damage control officer reported that a fire in the captain's cabin was being fought by members of the forward repair party assisted by crews of the adjacent 20-mm. guns and was under control. It was the one caused by the hit which had earlier stopped two 5-inch guns. He also reported that another hit received amidships had caused little damage.

With gunfire suspended, Moran's eyes recovered from flash blindness. At 12:06, when an urgent report came, he was able to see a short thin line of phosphorescent bubbles out on the starboard bow. It was a torpedo's wake! A torpedo was streaking through the water on a collision course with his ship. The absolute silence of its swift, stealthy advance was frightening. He shouted for hard right rudder, backed the starboard engine. The ship swung right.

"Torpedo approaching!" The word was passed to all stations. Men braced, held their breath.

In the first seconds it was impossible to tell whether the torpedo had been seen in time. Then the fast-moving line of bubbles swept out of sight under the swinging bow and reappeared on the port side, racing off into the dark. Again somebody called a warning, pointed excitedly.

A second track of bubbles, about parallel to the first but somewhat to the right and behind it, was bearing down on the twisting ship. It flashed along the starboard side, missing the rapidly swinging stern by no more than thirty yards. Quickly Moran reversed the rudder and steadied the ship. After a short pause in which no more tracks were seen he turned back to regain position in column. The news was received with relief, particularly below decks.

After disposing of the cruiser target which the main battery had shared with the secondary, *Helena* had begun searching for another. She was still searching when Scott's midnight order to cease firing was heard.

The search continued. Soon it was determined that a radar contact nine thousand yards on the starboard beam was an enemy ship trying to escape. She was tracked on a heading of northwest at a speed of thirty knots. The guns had already been trained on her when, at 12:04, flashes of gunfire were seen in the same direction.

Captain Hoover ordered both batteries to commence firing though Scott's order to cease fire still stood. Almost at once two groups of splashes were seen in quick succession to the left of one of the U.S. ships ahead. The splashes were apparently "overs" fired by the new target.

Helena fired at this ship at intervals, breaking off several times to check her aim. At 12:06 the wake of a torpedo coming from starboard shot across the bow at right angles only a few yards ahead. At 12:09 course was changed to the northwest to continue in the track of the ships ahead.

The flagship had apparently turned in that direction to maintain close contact with the enemy though no signal had been heard. This moved the target from the beam to the starboard bow. At least one of the U.S. cruisers was now shooting across *Helena*'s line of fire at something to the right of her target.

A searchlight beam ahead reached into the darkness to starboard. Then, without warning, a terrifying spectacle burst out. It was *Boise,* sheering to port, an intense fire enveloping her entire forecastle in flames that reached higher than her open bridge. Only burning ammunition could cause such a display. The scene looked like the prelude to total destruction.

Boise drew rapidly off from the column and dropped aft. In *Hel-*

ena's control stations the men were too busy to watch longer. The target *Helena* had been shooting at was finally seen when she burst into flames. Her appearance was soon followed by a heavy explosion. With this, the target and its radar pip vanished.

Now all firing had ceased. A strange quiet settled in. Neither *San Francisco* nor *Salt Lake City* could be seen. The task group commander was heard on TBS ordering a change of course to southwest. There were still pips in the SG scope but most could not be identified.

A sudden confrontation with an enemy was possible. Even more possible was a disastrous meeting between friends. Hoover came to the new course, proceeded warily at twenty knots. His lookouts were tense. A steady stream of information came from the SG, but things would have been easier had he been able to look at the scope himself.

In *Salt Lake City* the midnight order to cease firing had not been heard. Several ships were burning to starboard at this time. None was seen shooting. Lieutenant George O'Connell, controlling the main battery in the foretop, chose three ships showing the least amount of flame and took them under fire successively for a total of seven salvos. Then a repetition of Scott's order was heard and *Salt Lake City* ceased.

A lull followed, disturbed only by *Helena*. At 12:06 *Boise*'s maneuver to dodge torpedoes caused some tense searching but none were sighted. *Boise* had pulled ahead again when, at 12:10, the bluish beam of one of her searchlights cut through the dark and she burst into a long, rolling discharge of continuous fire.

Salt Lake City's gunners, in the meantime, had been watching a radar contact on the starboard quarter, one of the burning ships. Successive readings suggested that this ship might not be as badly injured as she appeared. She was making a respectable fifteen knots in a northwesterly direction and had to be assumed to be capable of continued fighting. *Boise* and *Helena* were shooting now. Though Captain Small had heard no further command from Scott, he ordered his gunnery officer to take the contact under fire.

Brewer was ready. The first two salvos fell short. The next two appeared to be hits. Then a bright glow of light from ahead caught his attention. He looked to see *Boise,* which had turned a little to the right, enveloped forward in a fierce blanket of fire and almost at once he saw the cause.

An enemy ship on the starboard bow which had gone unnoticed had pounced on the source of the searchlight beam. There was a small, quick, multiple flash in that direction. Almost at once, Brewer heard the unmistakable clang of a heavy missile striking *Boise's* steel plates. Another multiple flash followed, and soon another, as if the enemy had brought up a completely fresh ship. She was firing fast and she was hitting!

Boise's slight turn to the right had caused Small to put his rudder left to give her more room. Now *Boise* came sharply left, starting out of column toward the unengaged side. Small promptly reversed the rudder and backed the starboard engines, bringing his ship to the right to avoid a collision. Soon *Salt Lake City* was passing between *Boise* and the enemy, beautifully silhouetted by the former.

In the meantime, Brewer had shifted aim to deal with the ship on the starboard bow. Simultaneously, the main battery fired a salvo, the secondary let go a spread of star shell, and a searchlight was opened just for the time needed to see the first salvo fall. Then it was doused. The stars opened, revealing a cruiser. Four more salvos were fired. The target ceased firing after the first or second salvo. After the last, she disappeared. The time was 12:16.

Neither Small nor Brewer had seen what was happening closer at hand. In the blinding shock of their own guns they had not seen or heard the impact of projectiles upon their own ship. Now they began to receive reports.

Salt Lake City had been hit forward in the vicinity of the gasoline stowage. The automatic alarm system had incorrectly indicated a fire and the forward magazines were flooded by the damage control officer as a precaution. *Salt Lake City* had received a second hit which forced abandonment of several stations due to heat and smoke. Most important was a station in the ammunition train serving the forward 5-inch guns.

Before the significance of this information could be assessed, the bridge lost steering control. Control, however, was picked up quickly by the after steering station. But this was a precarious expedient in the middle of a battle. Orders for the rudder had to be relayed electrically over a vulnerable wire for more than half the length of the ship. On top of this Lieutenant Commander Theodore H. Kobey, the engineer officer, reported that the forward fire room was out of commission and the ship's maximum speed was reduced, for the present at least, to twenty-two knots.

There was now no sign of the enemy except for a dim, distant flicker of fire which was seen briefly to the northwest. By now, the U.S. force was so spread out that none of the other ships could be found by eye. There had been no shooting after *Salt Lake City* had ceased. To all appearances she was alone on a dark, quiet ocean.

Buchanan, McCalla, and *Laffey* were largely spectators at this stage of the battle. They all heard the order to cease firing at midnight. Only *McCalla,* near the end of the period, found a target, which seemed to be a destroyer, seventy-five hundred yards abeam. When an order to resume fire was heard on TBS at 12:12, she opened up at once. Immediately afterward, *Boise* flared up. *McCalla's* target did not return her fire and seemed to be running at reduced speed. She dropped slowly aft and in five minutes, burning brightly, she suddenly disappeared. She seemed to have sunk. Firing was checked. There was no more shooting by any ship. The three destroyers were in a strung-out column still following *Helena.*

In the first minutes after midnight Admiral Scott was again having difficulty making an order stick. Some of the ships were slow to cease firing. Still others seemed to have resumed their fire, though the order to cease was repeated several times. From the flag bridge no targets could be seen. *San Francisco's* gunners could find no target. And after twelve minutes, the formation still had not closed appreciably. In fact, judging from the flashes of gunfire astern, the formation was spreading farther out. At 12:12 a message came from Lieutenant Thomas in the *San Francisco* plane, last heard from at 11:30 over the Guadalcanal shore. He was now circling above. "I am over the disposition. Which way are you firing?"

Almost at once six tall splashes, tightly grouped, sprang into the air just beyond the flagship's stern. A few seconds later a second group flashed midway in the dark interval to *Boise*. The third and fourth groups followed in rapid succession. Somewhere a spotter was earning his pay! At one instant *Boise*'s forecastle was smothered in foam. In the next it flared up like a giant torch.

Scott gave the order to resume firing with the first splashes. *San Francisco*'s gunners had seen the quick, multiple flash in the dark to starboard when the first salvo had been fired. The radar had been brought to bear and found a contact a little abaft the beam at seven thousand yards. *Boise* was starting to pull out of the column to the disengaged side, her forecastle crowned with a huge, billowing mass of bright flame, her after turrets still firing, as *San Francisco*'s first salvo departed.

Star shell fired by another ship disclosed the target, a heavy cruiser. *San Francisco*'s first salvo missed. The second struck, causing a heavy explosion, the biggest observed at any time during the battle. Splashes around the cruiser indicated that at least one other American ship was firing at her.

Now radar found another contact, almost directly beyond. A few saw it briefly through the smoke and glare—too fleetingly to identify it. Using radar alone, the gunners sent several salvos in that direction without visible result. The contact was soon lost and fire was checked.

Returning to position in column after combing the torpedo wakes, *Boise* had found a radar contact near the starboard beam. It might have been the ship which had nearly torpedoed her. Using searchlight illumination as well as radar, she took the ship under continuous fire. Though the hard, unwavering searchlight continued to stare at the victim, it was difficult to identify her. Finally, a small fire broke out on the target.

Then the blow came. Splashes suddenly bracketed *Boise*'s bow. The volume of fire from the forward turrets diminished. Several of the nine 6-inch guns were no longer shooting. A report of a fire in Turret One had just been received on the open bridge when a shock knocked men to their knees. A huge cloud of burning gas and choking smoke billowed up from the forecastle. Debris, hot water, and sparks flew into the air. The blinding curtain obscured everything forward.

Lieutenant Commander William C. Butler, assistant gunnery officer, expected the final monstrous explosion to occur even as he heard the Captain shout through the voice tube for left rudder and thirty knots. The after turrets, as though in another world, continued to shoot as the ship swung. Earlier Moran had maneuvered to avoid torpedoes; now he was trying to shake off gunfire. Men at the after gunnery stations saw a last enemy salvo fall short, about where the ship would have been had she not pulled out. Then *Boise* ceased firing as the U.S. ships which had been astern drew between her and the target.

No final, monstrous explosion occurred. The holocaust diminished almost at once. It was possible to see the forecastle again from the open bridge though flames still roared from the apertures of Turrets One and Two. The fires gave off enough light to mark the ship miles away.

Moran had ordered the forward magazines flooded, but the remote controls did not seem to be working. He was told that the control panel lights showed the flood valves still closed.

Fire fighters from the repair parties were deployed on the forecastle as rapidly as the subsiding flames permitted. Some brought up hose to extinguish the fire still pouring from the turrets. Others put out small, scattered blazes left from the first, terrible outburst. Patches of deck planking continued to glow. A life raft lashed to the armored roof of Turret Two still smoldered.

The ship was down by the bow with a small list to starboard. Some spaces forward had flooded. Hopefully, they were the magazines— where the water would act to quench fire. Flooding to that extent would be fortunate. Much more would be serious.

Beyond the ship, the signs of battle had disappeared. *Boise* was alone with her own battle. The outcome depended largely on the skill and courage of the men in the repair parties. Moran reduced speed to twenty knots, retiring on a track which led south along the west shore of Guadalcanal. His destination was the morning rendezvous Scott had designated in his instructions. But between here and there lay an uncertain struggle with fire and flood, and the danger of a sudden encounter in the dark.

Peering through the fire which was raging forward, those still on their feet on *Duncan*'s bridge tried to detect any remaining signs of battle. To all appearances, however, the ship was completely alone. She was still steaming at fifteen knots, in a wide curve to the left.

The fire aft continued to burn fiercely; the bridge remained completely isolated from the rest of the ship. There were occasional sharp reports as 20-mm. ammunition cooked off in the ready boxes. It soon became obvious that the living would have to leave. At this point, there was more chance of surviving in the water, however dubious.

At Taylor's order, and under Lieutenant Commander Bryan's direction, the wounded were lowered from the control stations to the bridge. Smoke and flame stopped an effort to break out the life net stowed under the port wing. The entire port side of the bridge was getting hot.

The life jackets of the wounded were checked to insure that all were tied securely. Then these men were lowered into the water by line from the starboard wing, one at a time. Since the ship was still moving, they were widely separated. The able-bodied followed, sliding part way down a line, then dropping.

A half hour passed. Only Taylor and Bryan were left. Fire was closing in. It was no longer possible to step out on the port wing or even to stand within the port side of the pilothouse. Conditions were not much better on the starboard wing. A 20-mm. shell exploded occasionally. No escape to other parts of the ship was possible. The time in which a man could continue to survive on *Duncan*'s bridge had run out. The two officers shook hands and Bryan climbed over the side and disappeared. After a last, quick inspection, Taylor followed his executive officer.

In the first seconds after letting go, Taylor was engulfed in the dark, liquid silence of the ocean. The water was pleasantly warm. Then he surfaced and saw *Duncan*'s undamaged stern sweep by. The hull number, 485, painted on the side plating at the starboard quarter was conspicuous, the numerals still white and neat. The ship curved slowly off into the silent distance, marked by the light of her flames.

Floating easily in the calm water, Taylor watched her for a long while.

When *San Francisco* ceased firing, the whole battle area was suddenly quiet. Whatever the enemy's objective, he had been hit hard and had been turned back. Scott could see a couple of distant, waning fires but no other sign of any ship. *San Francisco* had apparently moved out well ahead of her own formation. *Boise* was in trouble if she was still afloat. The fate of Tobin's destroyers was in doubt. The task group was too disorganized to continue the pursuit of what was left of the enemy. At 12:20 Scott broadcast another order to cease firing. He directed *San Francisco* to take a course to the southwest, breaking off the engagement and establishing a heading which would facilitate the regrouping of his ships. Despite several repetitions of the order for this movement, there was no acknowledgment from *Boise, Farenholt,* or *Duncan*. Scott ordered *McCalla* to turn back and search for *Boise*. The search might also turn up one of the missing destroyers.

Now the process of sighting, recognizing, and forming up would begin. Even this would have its perils. There was no certainty that an enemy ship, perhaps a cripple which could still strike, was not in the vicinity. There was always the possibility that an enemy submarine was near, attracted by the gunfire and looking now for a likely target. And all hands were suddenly dog-tired. There was a natural tendency to let down one's guard. But the penalties for carelessness were obvious to all. From captain to seaman, tension remained high.

Flashing recognition lights occasionally, *Helena, Salt Lake City,* and the two remaining destroyers followed separate tracks. Each should converge gradually upon *San Francisco*'s. Aboard *Salt Lake City* the lights of three ships had been seen but the ships themselves could not be recognized because of distance.

At 12:44 Scott's order was heard loud and clear on TBS: "Stand by for further action. The show may not be over." Three minutes later he ordered the ships to flash recognition lights again.

As *Salt Lake City* flashed hers, a lookout sighted a shape to starboard. Small, Brewer, and others quickly found it, too distant to be recognized in the dark. With a start they noticed that it remained completely blackened, making no sign of recognition at all. *Salt Lake City*'s guns were immediately trained out.

Another order came from Scott: "Stop flashing recognition lights and close this ship."

Which was "this ship?" Did the Admiral's picture include the sleeper to starboard?

"All turrets load!" Ten 8-inch shells were rammed home, the powder bags shoved in behind. The guns were still red hot.

"Commence firing!"

Two 5-inch guns recoiled with a bright, incandescent boom. Each ejected an empty cartridge case from the breach. Each case was scooped up fast and tossed aside by a man wearing large, asbestos mitts.

It took an unbearably long time for the stars to open. Every gun, every telescope, every pair of binoculars was aimed in one direction. The man at the main battery firing key pressed his head hard against the buffer at the eyepiece of his telescope. His finger was on the triggerlike switch, ready to squeeze.

"Cease firing! Cease firing!" The order was followed by loud exclamations of relief.

Three small glowing objects, two green and one white, had just been fired from the target by a Very pistol, a pyrotechnic signaling device. Next, the stranger flashed her recognition lights, green over green over white. Finally, the 5-inch stars opened behind her, revealing *San Francisco*. A contact in the switch controlling her recognition lights, loosened by the shock of gunfire, had almost caused a calamity.

American nerves need not have been so taut. At 12:20 *Aoba, Kinugasa,* and *Hatsuyuki* were speeding northwest by the route they had come, straining to throw off pursuit and reach the two-hundred-mile mark as rapidly as possible. *Kinugasa* had been busy in the later stages of the battle. Her torpedoes were probably the ones which almost hit *Boise* and *Helena,* her guns probably those that nearly destroyed *Boise* and damaged *Salt Lake City.* She had taken no punishment in return.

There is no record of what *Hatsuyuki* did after turning around but she, too, escaped damage. *Aoba* was too badly hit at the beginning to take an effective part in the action. *Furutaka,* now straggling behind the others, had been mortally hurt. Multiple gun hits and possibly one or more hits by torpedoes fired by *Duncan* or *Buchanan* or both were hurrying *Furutaka*'s end. She was probably the ship caught in *Boise*'s searchlight beam and gunfire just before the latter's spectacular ordeal. It was probably she who, in return, had inflicted several 5-inch hits causing minor damage in *Boise*. All that remained of *Fubuki* was her survivors, an unseen cluster of flotsam on the dark surface of the ocean.

The American ships formed column astern of *San Francisco* and the reduced task group started to retire. All hands remained at battle stations, tired but exhilarated by the knowledge that American gunners had done something to redeem the debacle at the Battle of Savo Island.

Sandwiches and coffee were distributed from the galleys. Lieutenant Thomas was ordered to land his plane at Tulagi. There was time to reflect, and the few who had had an opportunity to see the action tried again to assess what they had seen.

Scott, after discussion with McMorris and others, sent a message at 2:28 to Comsopac reporting results. He estimated that at least four enemy destroyers and possibly a cruiser had been sunk or disabled and noted his missing ships. He requested air cover at daylight.

The message was just sent off when a welcome call came via TBS. It was *Boise*. She was several miles away and had the task group in her SG radar scope. She approached from the port quarter and finally slipped into her old position astern of *San Francisco*. Scrutinizing her closely, Scott was amazed that the dark outlines of her forecastle and superstructure had suffered no apparent change, though Turrets One and Two were still trained to starboard.

A little later a message to the Commanding General, Guadalcanal, was intercepted. It directed that air cover be provided as requested and that an air search for enemy stragglers start at dawn.

Though *Boise* was back, her plane was not. Since 11:30 Lieutenant (jg) R. C. Bartlett and his observer had been bobbing on the ocean in their disabled craft. They could see Savo Island to the east.

They had seen the firing to westward but had no certainty of the outcome. Their engine was quite dead and they could only wait for daylight, hoping that friendly eyes would see them. They were waiting patiently when, at 2:30, they saw a shape emerging from the gloom to the east. It looked as if it would pass close enough to see them. It was not likely to be friendly. Their fears mounted when a second and then a third shape appeared, following in the wake of the first. The aviators watched them pass, one behind the other, like sleepwalkers. They were headed west, running at perhaps eighteen knots. Staring into the darkness after the last ship, Bartlett thought he had seen a destroyer and two larger ships, at least one of which was a small cruiser. He was able to report this at Henderson Field later the same day.

Chapter Eight

OF FIRE AND FLOOD

A BATTLE IS USUALLY CONSIDERED ENDED when the shooting stops. In a ship, however, it is sometimes just beginning. Starting as an encounter with a military foe, it often becomes a struggle with completely impersonal forces. The first enemy, other men fighting with weapons that cause fire and flood, is displaced by fire and flood themselves.

Boise was hit seven times in the shooting that occurred after she successfully evaded the Japanese torpedoes. Four or five of the hits came from the ship that was her target near the starboard beam. This count was based on the position of certain shell holes found later, as well as other evidence. These holes had been made by 5-inch projectiles. The other hits were made by the ship on the starboard bow with 8-inch. One shell—size and source undetermined—exploded on the face plate of Turret Three. One of the 8-inch hits almost finished *Boise,* but first there was trouble in Turret One.

That turret, with the rest of the main battery, was shooting in continuous fire at the target near the starboard beam. The bearing was drawing aft and the turret was very slowly revolving in that direction to keep on target. Suddenly the turret stopped turning. No unusual blow had been felt. The turret officer immediately ceased fire. The turret would not turn left, either, and seemed to be jammed. The interior was suddenly filled with heavy, choking smoke. As the men tried to find the trouble, they heard a fizzing sound. The turret officer ordered the turret abandoned and reported the situation by telephone.

The left hatch in the bottom side of the overhang at the rear of the turret was opened, providing an exit for one man at a time. (The right hatch was never opened.) Each lowered himself through the hole, coughing and choking, dropped to his knees on the forecastle

100

deck, sucked in a breath of fresh air, and scrambled clear of the over-hang. The first few had barely regained their feet when a burst of flame shot up from Turret Two.

Reacting automatically, the men raced for safety, stumbling over the anchor chain, stopping only when they reached the triangle at the extreme bow between the hawse pipes. Looking back, they saw a thick tongue of incandescent gas blowing from the opening in Turret One through which they had just dropped. It had ignited the deck planking beneath. Flames rose with a deep shuddering sound, boiling up from Turrets One and Two through the gun apertures and other openings. The heat in the eyes of the ship, where these few survivors of Turret One were penned, was almost unbearable. Nothing could be seen beyond the fire; nothing seemed even to exist beyond the fire. The continued swishing of the water past the bows had a ghostly quality, as though the forward end of the ship had parted from the rest and were moving under its own power. Eleven men had reached the eyes of the ship. Some were burned and did not know it yet.

When a ship is hit, the damage received directly may be minor compared with what follows. Fire and flooding may proceed rather slowly but spread surely, finally destroying the ship. On the other hand, prompt action taken by trained men may save a dangerous situation. All U.S. ships had several repair parties, groups of men specially instructed in fire fighting, shoring bulkheads, patching holes, and taking other emergency measures to keep the ship afloat and fighting. They made up the nucleus of the damage control organization. The damage control officer coordinated their efforts from his post at a place called central station.

Boise's amidships repair party was sent forward when the forward repair party failed to respond. Shortly afterward Commander Burtnett K. Culver, the executive officer, hurried forward.

He found men already advancing onto the forecastle. Some were hosing down smoking planking, others trying to enter Turrets One and Two, each frozen in the position in which it had fired its last shot. A hose was shoved into the left hatch of Turret One. It was still burning inside and too hot to enter. When the hatches of Turret Two were opened, they were found blocked with bodies. Hoses were inserted through the powder case ejector openings.

On the deck below, the wardroom was full of suffocating smoke. Just outside, Culver found men at a door tending a line. At the other end, somewhere forward, a man wearing a rescue breathing apparatus was exploring the damage.

Lieutenant (jg) T. D. Morris came up, reported he had tried to open the forward magazine flood valves from the remote electric control panel. But almost overcome by smoke, he had been unable to get a response from the indicator lights. Then he had sent a man with a rescue breather to the panel. He, in turn, had pushed the switches several more times with no better result.

Whether the valves had opened or not, the forward magazines soon were flooded. The worst of the fire quickly subsided. As the smoke below decks cleared, men gingerly unscrewed the caps from the sounding tubes extending into the magazines and found them full of water. An instrument like a carpenter's level in central station showed that the ship was down by the bow, confirming what one could already feel.

In the next two and a half hours the extent of the flooding was fully determined and measures started to prevent its spread. All fires were put out. The surgeon, forced from the battle dressing station in the wardroom by smoke, treated thirty-five wounded in a makeshift station in the galley. The removal of the dead from the burned-out turrets commenced.

Boise settled at a draft of 27' 9" forward and 20' 6" aft. Her damage control officer, Lieutenant Commander Thomas M. Wolverton, estimated she had shipped twelve hundred tons of water. To cope with this, twenty portable electric submersible pumps, energized from the casualty power system, were lowered into the flooded spaces. Hose was led topside and overboard, and the long job of pumping began.

Only when *Boise* was finally drydocked did a complete explanation emerge for what had happened. An 8-inch shell had struck Number One Barbette (the armored cylinder on which Turret One turned) at a spot just above the main deck. It failed to penetrate completely and stuck between the barbette and the rotating part of the turret inside, jamming the latter.

Its high-explosive charge, instead of detonating, burned noisily but harmlessly, and it was this jamming and the heavy smoke which started the evacuation of the turret. At nearly the same time a second shell, later found to have been of the flat-nosed type, struck the water short of the ship, traveled a short distance submerged, pierced the hull nine feet below the water line, and exploded in the magazine separating the handling rooms under Turrets One and Two.

Fragments of it penetrated into both handling rooms, some reached the magazine between the handling rooms under Turrets Two and Three, and one even entered the handling room under Turret Three. The exposed charges of powder in the handling rooms of Turrets One and Two and the magazines which had been penetrated were immediately ignited. The gas pressures generated were too much for the flameproof barriers and the fire flashed up the ammunition train to the gun chambers of the two forward turrets.

All who were caught in its path—all hands except the eleven who had just left Turret One—were killed. Flame entered the handling room under Turret Three through the single small hole in the forward bulkhead. Only one man was burned and exposed powder was shielded in time. In the magazine in which the shell exploded the closures of the ventilating ducts were blown open, permitting burning gas to rush up the ducts. It burst them at the second deck in the vicinity of the wardroom and blew out upon the men of the forward repair party there, killing them instantly and filling the entire area with heavy smoke.

Two circumstances prevented the quickly mounting rate of combustion from reaching irresistible proportions. First, in accordance with long-established practice and regulation, only a minimum amount of powder was exposed in the magazines, handling rooms, and gun chambers. Second, the shell which caused the fire also provided the means for putting it out. The sea poured in through the large, jagged hole in the hull and through the same shrapnel holes which had permitted the spread of fire.

The electrical system which operated the flood valves had been damaged and they never did open. It was not necessary. The water poured in rapidly and put out the fire quickly. As evidence of this, the rubber covering of the portable telephone cords which were later found in the damaged handling rooms was still in good condition.

The gunnery officer, Lieutenant Commander John J. Laffan, estimated that about three thousand pounds of powder burned. None in the storage tanks, where the bulk of the powder was kept, had been disturbed.

Salt Lake City's wounds were not as severe as *Boise*'s. Still, her damage control crews, engineers, and electricians worked through the night and beyond. Up to the time that *Salt Lake City* was silhouetted between the burning *Boise* and the enemy, nothing unusual had occurred at the forward distribution board—the electric power station for the forward part of the ship. Then Warrant Electrician A. J. Squires, the officer in charge, felt an impact—one different from the usual shocks caused by the ship's guns. Squires and his helpers knew at once it was a hit. They scanned the board, but no circuit breakers had opened, no meters were reading abnormally. Then word came through the phones from the engineers' repair party: "Hit, starboard side, forward fire room! Secure all power forward on starboard side!"

This was the kind of situation they had drilled for many times in "battle problems." Instantly, a man went down the length of the board pulling certain switches. Another man applied some test apparatus to two of the switches which had been opened. "No shorts," he reported.

The two switches were closed again.

"Power restored to Turret One and forward five-inch ammunition hoists," reported the talker into his phones.

By this time the forward fire room had been abandoned. The hatch was closed down upon the roar of escaping steam and the smell of an oil fire. It had been a narrow escape. The fire room crew did not understand what had happened until they saw the hole in the second deck over the top of the fire room.

An 8-inch shell had come through the starboard side of the ship and had crashed through the second deck, despite the thickness of its armor. But in doing so it had spent all its energy; it dropped into the fire room impelled only by the force of gravity, bumping the piping in its path as it fell. At the bottom it hit a deck plate in front of Number One Boiler and exploded with a loud report. One man, standing almost next to the explosion, was killed. The others—some within six feet—suffered no injury at all. A huge, trembling tuft of steam blew from a hole in the auxiliary steam line with a deafening rush. The explosion was nevertheless of a low order because of some defect in the shell.

The men were quickly driven out of the fire room. As soon as they reached the second deck a couple of them hurried to the remote control and closed the valve which isolated the section in the forward fire room from the rest of the auxiliary steam line.

Once steam stopped blowing from the hole in the second deck, they could see that there was still a fire to be reckoned with. Chief Warrant Officer Ivan Rich, the boiler division officer, led a party with fire-fighting gear back into the fire room. They fought the fire for a few minutes, but were turned back by heat and smoke. The fire was being fed by a broken fuel connection whose supply could not be turned off.

While Captain Small on the bridge was searching for *San Francisco,* Lieutenant Commander Kobey and his men on the hot deck over the fire room were searching their minds for a way to put out the fire. One possibility was worth a try.

The same valve which had been closed a few minutes earlier was opened again. Steam poured in from aft through the break in the line made by the exploding shell. The steam filled the forward fire room, displaced the air, enveloped the flames, and finally smothered them completely.

For Rich and some of his men this was the real start of the battle. An engineer does not rest until every piece of damaged machinery capable of being restored is running again.

In the forward fire room the boilers had to be closely inspected, damaged machinery repaired, holes patched, and the mess caused by fire cleaned up before the present maximum speed of twenty-two knots could be increased. That increase might prove to be the essential margin in another encounter with the same ships, a submarine, or an aircraft. Speed was as much a part of the ship's fighting ability as was fire power. Systematically Rich assigned the jobs. The men went to work as though this were the 8 A.M. "turn-to" alongside a dock at a navy yard.

Aboard *Farenholt,* flooding had succeeded the Japanese as the enemy. After the last hit, speed was reduced to five knots, but in two or three minutes the engineers were able to make twenty-five. But now there were other problems.

Several compartments, including the forward fire room, were flooded. Their bulkheads, already under pressure from the water, might not be able to take the additional pressures of higher speeds.

Farenholt was listing five degrees to port. The effectiveness of her guns was severely reduced by the lack of centralized control. Captain Seaward decided to continue at five knots pending a more thorough survey of the damage.

Repair operations now turned into a holding action in defense of the ship's remaining buoyancy and stability. The work called for special knowledge, ingenuity, hard work, and nerve. The whole effort was led by the repair parties, assisted by gunners and engineers drawn temporarily from their normal stations.

Everybody aboard knew Archimedes' principle, that a floating body sinks to a depth at which it displaces an equal weight of water. For officers and men the implications were clear. A flooded compartment added tons to the weight of the ship, inches to its draft, and reduced its ability to right itself when rolled in the trough of the sea.

The first concern in *Farenholt* was that the bulkheads of the flooded spaces would contain their loads and not give way or spring leaks which would flood the adjacent spaces. The second, and less pressing, was the five-degree list to port, caused by the larger quantity of sea water on that side.

When Lieutenant Commander Beckmann came to inspect the damage, he found the forward repair party already starting to shore up threatened bulkheads. Flashing a light down the forward fireroom hatch, he saw that the water was at the level of the upper grating.

In the forward engine room the men were watching their own forward bulkhead closely. It was all that separated them from the water standing in the forward fire room a dozen feet higher than their own bilges. They had already plugged a few small holes made by flying shrapnel and now were inspecting seams and fittings where cable and piping passed through from the flooded space. So far, everything remained tight.

Beckmann talked with Seaward on the bridge, then returned to the main deck. At his direction men were taken from gun stations. Damaged equipment such as the boat was dropped overboard. Other material was moved from port to starboard. The speed of the ship was cautiously increased until there was enough to roll the depth charges safely over the stern. They were dropped one after the other, set not to go off, though two did anyway. The 43 wounded, four in serious condition, were cared for. (Three others had been killed.) There was no doctor on board. The medical department's senior man, a chief pharmacist's mate, was badly wounded himself. His assistant, a second class, took over and was helped by several men of other departments who had received advanced first-aid instruction several months before.

In the meantime, Seaward was steering in the general direction of the morning rendezvous. With recovery measures underway, Beckmann returned to the bridge to pick up his duties as navigator. Men not engaged in damage-control tasks remained alert for another encounter.

The battle against the Japanese had long since ended. Tobin and Seaward thought the enemy had been repulsed but were concerned with the possibility that *Farenholt's* identity could be mistaken by friends also retiring toward the rendezvous. The Very pistol which would fire the emergency recognition signal was ready.

When the ship had finally been brought to an even keel, putting the hole in the port side of the forward fire room near the water line again, it became apparent that it might be possible to empty that space. There were pumps which could be used if the valve in the bilges of the fire room could be opened. But now, as a result of battle damage, the valve could not be operated from the remote control topside.

The only way to open it was to go down, twelve feet under water, under projecting gratings, behind machinery, in total darkness. There was diving equipment on board. But something like this could be dangerous at any time. For tired, edgy men, just finished with one battle and aware that another could start at any time, the prospect of going under water now to close this valve was forbidding.

Lieutenant (jg) Keller volunteered. His nerve was soon rewarded and pumping started at once. By daylight much of the water had been pulled out with a corresponding gain in buoyancy. In addition, a list of nine degrees to starboard was deliberately put on to keep the hole above water, and speed was increased to twenty knots.

When *McCalla* received the order early on the twelfth to search for *Boise,* Captain Cooper immediately reversed course. He headed back toward the spot at which he had last seen *Boise,* a ball of fire burning a bright hole in the night. When he reached that point, he found nothing. He decided to sweep the area as thoroughly as possible. *Boise,* or a part of her, might still be floating. Or perhaps some survivors might be adrift in the dark.

A careful watch would have to be kept not only ahead and to the sides, but also down into the water near the ship. The watch would have to include listening as well as looking. *McCalla* might find friendly life rafts. She might just as easily find an enemy ship engaged in a similar rescue mission.

McCalla had been searching for some time when a fire was sighted to the southeast. She turned toward it. As she drew closer, a stricken ship could be seen. This was definitely not *Boise.* The hulk lay dead in the water, her forward half engulfed in a covering of smoke and flame. She seemed to have only one stack.

The outline of Savo Island was visible to one side and several miles beyond. After circling cautiously and seeing no sign of life, Cooper ordered Lieutenant Commander Myhre to organize and lead a boarding party. He was to make positive identification, take any action that might be desirable and possible, and wait for the return of *McCalla* which would continue searching for *Boise.* In the event *McCalla* did not return, he was to go to Tulagi.

The boarding party was mustered and lowered in a motor whaleboat at 3:00 A.M. Besides Myhre the group included Lieutenant (jg) Weems, Chief Pharmacist's Mate Luna, Second Class Signalman Fyock, Third Class Gunner's Mate Nichols, Seamen Giegerich and Reaves, and Fireman Baker.

McCalla disappeared at once into the dark and Myhre, with his little command, was on his own. He turned toward the burning ship, closing at low speed, and stopped two or three times to listen. There was no sound except for an occasional crackling which seemed to be small-caliber ammunition exploding. He was still unable to identify the wreck. The after part looked intact and might contain a few able-bodied men, possibly Japanese.

Two hundred yards from the stern the boat was stopped again. Weems removed his clothes, donned both a kapok and a pneumatic life jacket, and slipped over the side. He rode high, paddling easily and quietly across the calm, dark water. He paused several times.

From a point fifty yards off the port quarter, he thought he saw the outline of a sentry on deck holding a rifle in readiness. The figure remained motionless for so long that he finally decided it was something inanimate. He closed half the remaining distance and recognized the figure as a davit.

At the same time he saw with a shock the numerals 485, white and unblemished, standing out on the dark side at the ship's quarter. The fire forward, the profound stillness aft, were ominous. He hailed the ship but there was no response. He tried to board by climbing up the port propeller guard but a starboard list put it too high to reach. He finally swam around the stern and climbed up to the starboard guard, which was correspondingly lower.

Slipping under the life line, he glanced around the fantail. On deck a limp hose ran forward from a fire plug. There was no sign of life. He hailed the boat loudly and called it alongside.

When the rest of the party arrived, they inspected the topside of the ship, or as much of it as they could reach. They could move only as far forward as the area under the bridge.

What originally had been a single, huge conflagration had finally dwindled down into a number of smaller fires. The heat had buckled steel decks and melted steel fittings in places. The forward stack was gone, knocked completely over the side, and a section of deck over the forward fire room had been blown open. There were several corpses, some still burning, where men had fallen.

Myhre, flashing a light into the executive officer's room, was surprised to see a sword in its scorched scabbard still in a rack on the bulkhead. It had been presented to Lieutenant Commander Bryan as the outstanding athlete at the Naval Academy in the Class of 1932. Weems, now here with Myhre, had won the same award ten years later.

Finding no one alive, the party returned to the fantail. The disconcerting popping of 20-mm. ammunition continued and the possibility of a 5-inch magazine going up could not be overlooked. Furthermore the fire might attract an enemy ship as *McCalla* had been attracted. In any event, little could be done while it was still dark. The boarding party climbed down into its boat, pulled a short distance away, and stopped the engine to wait for daylight.

The flames continued to flicker across the water, offering no clue as to what had become of the rest of *Duncan's* men.

Chapter Nine

THE NEXT MORNING

THE FIVE-SHIP JAPANESE SUPPORT GROUP that fought at Cape Esperance was perhaps one of the shortest lived tactical units in the history of the Imperial Navy. It dissolved at the start of the battle, never to form again. Eighth Fleet Headquarters was early notified by *Kinugasa* that a battle had been fought. *Hatsuyuki* was sent back to find *Furutaka*. At 2:08 she discovered the stricken cruiser, and none too soon. Twenty minutes later *Furutaka* sank, twenty-two miles northwest of Savo Island and forty-five miles from Henderson Field.

The Reinforcement Group unloading along the Guadalcanal north shore had seen the light and heard the rumble of distant battle. After the shooting stopped, *Nisshin* sent an inquiry to the commander of the Support Force but received no answer. A little after one o'clock the unloading job was done. All personnel and equipment had been safely landed.

The Reinforcement Group had not been disturbed and it was hoped that the enemy, whose nature was still unknown, had been defeated. The ships got under way and proceeded to a rendezvous beyond Cape Esperance where they would resume formation. (No disabled plane was seen on the water as they departed.)

Nothing unusual was seen except a fire to the north of Savo Island. *Nisshin*'s captain did not send a destroyer to investigate. In the uncertain circumstances he preferred to keep his force concentrated. (Several possibilities for *McCalla* and for Myhre and his party were thus ruled out.)

Half an hour later *Nisshin* received orders to send ahead destroyers *Asagumo* and *Natsugumo* to join *Kinugasa,* which had already reversed course and was coming back. Apparently, she was to protect the Reinforcement Group if necessary.

The meeting never took place. The headquarters at Rabaul, looking forward to daylight, seems to have decided within the hour that the approaching air threat outweighed every other consideration. The orders were changed. *Kinugasa* turned about and resumed her race up the Slot. The two destroyers returned to the Reinforcement Group.

Two more of *Nisshin's* destroyers, *Shirayuki* and *Murakumo,* were also detached about this time. Their mission was probably to search for survivors of *Fubuki.** While these events were taking place, *Aoba's* radio was repaired. At 2:45 she made her first report to Eighth Fleet Headquarters, including the first news of Admiral Goto's condition.

Long before the first sign of daylight, the throb of aircraft engines could be heard in the jungle beyond Henderson Field. It had been a good night for the defenders, undisturbed by enemy attack of any kind. Men who had been on duty around midnight had seen flashes in the sky to the northwest and heard the distant, hollow reverberations of heavy guns. The order for special morning operations had been received later and acted upon at once.

Squadron personnel were routed out of their muddy tents, planes armed, engines warmed up, missions assigned, and pilots briefed. As usual, necessity dictated a motley collection of planes for the tasks.

An attack group was formed under Marine Lieutenant Colonel Cooley. The force consisted of 11 Marine dive bombers, 6 Navy dive bombers, 16 Marine fighters, and 8 Army fighters. The Navy planes were at Henderson by chance. They were a part of Squadron VS-71 which had survived the sinking of the carrier *Wasp* by an enemy submarine the previous month.

At 5:20 the planes started taking off, their mission to find and attack Japanese stragglers from the previous night's battle. Cooley set course up the Slot, assembling his force on the way so as not to lose time. The sun was just rising when two ships were sighted five miles north of the Russell Islands. They were steaming in column at high

---

* Japanese records are incomplete regarding the movements of their ships on October 12. By comparing them with those of U.S. units which were engaged the same day, a plausible account can be constructed which will serve until better evidence appears.

speed, leaving a foamy wake which looked from the planes like a thin, white thread on the hazy blue carpet of the sea.

Their course, a little south of west, would lead them to a track along the south side of New Georgia and Rendova islands. This was an alternate route to the Japanese base at the lower end of Bougainville. The ships were quickly identified as enemy destroyers.

Cooley paused to divide his force. He sent Lieutenant Commander John Eldridge, commanding VS-71, with the Navy bombers and some of the fighters to search farther up the Slot. Then Cooley led his bombers up and into position for attack.

One at a time, they descended on the destroyers in steep power dives. The two ships had taken advantage of Cooley's delay to spread apart, making room for independent maneuvering. Now they twisted and turned desperately at top speed, forcing the descending planes to twist in an effort to hold the ships in their sights.

At the same time, the destroyers sent up a barrage of antiaircraft fire through which the attack had to be pressed. When it was over the pilots had seen several near misses and one of the ships seemed to be smoking as if it had been hit. Neither ship, however, had been slowed, and they soon resumed their course.

Eldridge and his dive bombers continued 90 more miles to a point nearly abreast the northwest tip of Santa Isabel Island. Here they sighted a single ship speeding northwest and recognized her as another enemy destroyer. Her violent maneuvers and a broken layer of clouds at fifteen hundred feet hindered the attack and nothing better than a near miss was seen. Bombs gone, the planes turned back, arriving at Henderson without seeing any further sign of stragglers.

After his group had completed its attack and expended its bombs, Cooley sent three of the planes to search ahead in the direction the pair of fleeing destroyers was taking. If the only objective of these ships was the quickest possible return to base, they should have been running northwest, through the Slot, passing New Georgia on the north side.

Instead, their present course would take them south of New Georgia and Rendova and add another forty miles to their trip. The discrepancy was enough to arouse curiosity. Cooley's other planes scouted the lower end of the Slot before going home. One of them went back for another look at the two destroyers and found them half an hour after the attack still on the same course but running at much lower speed. One was leaving a long, conspicuous track of oil. It looked as if the attack had not been completely unsuccessful.

At 7:50 the three planes which continued out on the route south of New Georgia made a discovery which justified Cooley's hunch. About six miles south of Rendova and 170 from Henderson Field, they sighted an enemy force of four destroyers and two larger ships that looked like cruisers. The formation was steaming at what was thought to be medium speed on a northwesterly course. One of the cruisers was trailing oil.*

The planes, however, could not attack and the state of their fuel supply soon forced them to depart. When their report reached Henderson Field it became apparent that at least two enemy cruisers and seven destroyers were retiring in three widely separated groups.

By daylight the same morning most of U.S. Task Group 64.2 was south of Guadalcanal enroute to Espiritu Santo. The combat air patrol from Henderson Field reported overhead. All ships released their men from battle stations and resumed normal watches.

Aboard *Boise* the submersible pumps continued slowly to bring down the water level in flooded spaces. As holes were found they were stopped with plugs, mattresses, and other expedients, but the job could not be completed at sea. The process was not speeded, either, by three submarine alarms in the first hours after dawn, nor by the interruptions incident to the discovery and disposition of corpses.

Repairs also were being made aboard *Salt Lake City*. Her crew was salvaging the machinery in her forward fire room and expected to restore two of the four boilers there. (This was accomplished late the same afternoon. The other two boilers could be repaired only in a navy yard.)

A message had been received from *Farenholt* reporting her location and condition. Only fifty miles astern, she was making good

---

* A ship can leak very little oil in making a track visible for miles from the air. This much can come from routine causes such as pumping bilges, or a few rivets in oil tanks suffering from old age rather than recent battle damage.

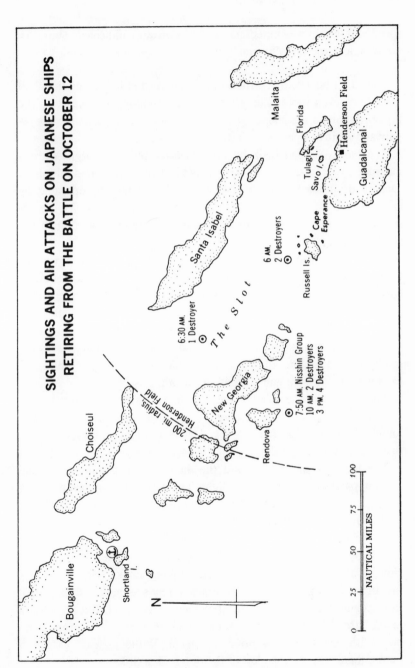

SIGHTINGS AND AIR ATTACKS ON JAPANESE SHIPS RETIRING FROM THE BATTLE ON OCTOBER 12

speed and was in no immediate need of assistance. The only ship now unaccounted for was *Duncan*.

McCalla's boat had returned to *Duncan* at first light. The fires had died down even more. The popping of ammunition had ceased. The boarding party's confidence increased. *Duncan* might be saved if repair and control operations were started fast.

The party climbed back on board with a plan. To begin with, a measure of defense had to be provided. There was ammunition at each of the after 5-inch guns, both of which could be operated by hand. Three 20-mm. guns were also supplied and ready. Myhre assigned stations at some of this armament, but the party was much too small to man all of it.

Present indications notwithstanding, the men knew the ship might take a sudden turn for the worse and sink before they could get clear. One of the first precautions taken was the setting of the depth charges. If the ship should sink, carrying them down, they would explode at the depth for which set, killing anyone floating nearby on the surface. This had happened before and it was something destroyer sailors seldom forgot. All of *Duncan*'s charges were now set on "safe" to prevent them from going off at any depth.

Next the boarding party turned to more positive measures. The men inspected the whole interior of the after part of the ship and found it undamaged. They checked all watertight fittings to insure they were closed.

The intensity of the fire and the damage it had caused became more apparent in the increasing light. The main deck amidships was a series of crazy waves. The paint had been burned off all the surfaces in the area. The remains of a couple of portable carbon dioxide fire extinguishers were identified. They were melted out of shape.

Soberly Myhre and his men observed the scene. The signs were obvious. There had been searing heat, choking smoke, exploding ammunition. The forward fire room was severely scorched and damaged. Both engine rooms and the after fire room were intact. But the boilers in the after fire room had at some moment, for some reason, gone out. With that there was no more steam. Without steam to run a pump, there was no hope left of fighting such a fire.

Fire still burned in spaces below the forecastle. Also, there was flooding somewhere forward. This was apparent from the fact that the ship was down at the bow by a moderate amount; it was also listing to starboard as first noticed by Lieutenant (jg) Weems.

Duncan's "handybilly," a portable gasoline-driven pump, was discovered aft. Alone it could not have been effective against the huge fire raging earlier. Now, however, it might help. It was brought up to the forecastle and a hose was attached to the suction side and dropped overboard. Another hose, attached to the discharge side, was led down a hatch and into the chief petty officers' quarters where fires were still strong and dangerously close to the forward magazines.

Adding more water to what was already in the ship would not make her more seaworthy. But it was a risk that had to be taken. Work was begun on plugging holes that could be reached, starting with those closest to the water line. If the ship started to settle further, submerging holes which had not been stopped up, flooding would accelerate and perhaps become unmanageable.

There were holes on both sides of the ship starting at the forward fire room and extending forward. Aside from those that were obviously caused by the passage of shells (some as large as 8-inch), there were many small ones punched out by shrapnel and flying debris.

Wooden plugs found in the damage-control locker aft, large quantities of mattresses, blankets, plus some life jackets, were used as stuffing material. The draft marks at either end of the ship were inspected frequently to insure that any marked increase in the rate of flooding would be spotted quickly.

Some small leaks near the bottom of the forward bulkhead of the forward fire room made it clear that the spaces immediately forward were flooded. Although an effort was made to shore the bulkhead, the job could not be done properly. There was too little timber and no satisfactory substitutes available and the interior was still sizzling hot from the flames that had gutted it.

These tasks weren't all started at once, nor did they continue uninterrupted. At about six o'clock aircraft were heard and all hands were hastily summoned to the guns. The planes, however, were soon recognized as friendly and the men returned to their labors. After two or three such alarms had interrupted work, Myhre decided to ignore the possibility of air attack.

Shortly after the first alarm *McCalla* was seen returning. When she drew within signaling range Myhre sent a message reporting that *Duncan* might be saved and requesting more men. By that time, however, *McCalla* was already busy rescuing men who had just been sighted in the water. For the time being, Myhre would have to do the best he could with his present strength.

At about 6:30, a patrol aircraft from Henderson Field reported a U.S. destroyer smoldering and dead in the water north of Savo Island. A second U.S. destroyer, also stopped but apparently undamaged, was in the same vicinity. The pilot, coming down low, saw the second ship haul a man out of the water. He called the field, reporting what he had seen. At about the same time *McCalla*'s skipper, Cooper, radioed, asking assistance. Additional aircraft and landing craft were soon dispatched to the scene.

McCalla's method of recovering able-bodied men was to come close and stop. The men did the rest. They swam alongside and climbed up a cargo net draped over the destroyer's side.

Often as one was recovered, others would be sighted. Sometimes the survivors were in small groups. The largest contained thirty-one in three life rafts which had been lashed together.

McCalla recovered the first man at 6:30 and the operation continued until afternoon. *McCalla* was drawing farther away from *Duncan* all the time. Aircraft overhead kept the destroyer moving continuously to recover newly discovered men. The landing craft, which traveled twenty-five miles to the scene, took over a share of the work as soon as they arrived in the forenoon. Cooper estimated the survivors were scattered over an area extending eight miles in a north and south direction and two east and west. They were, of course, from *Duncan*.

One great advantage in going into the water in this latitude was its balmy temperature, eighty degrees or more. The prospect of dying in a matter of minutes through loss of body heat was nonexistent.

On the other hand, there were distinct if less immediate hazards. One was prolonged exposure to the sun. Another was sharks. While *McCalla* was picking up one man, a second was observed under attack by a large shark two hundred yards to starboard. The fish made a series of rushes like a trout striking at a lure. Body and fins were clearly visible as the monster circled and lunged.

Cooper lowered a boat and stationed three men with rifles over the pilothouse to do what they could do. Perhaps a shark can seldom be stopped by rifle fire, but this time, at least, it might have been what did the trick.

When the boat reached the shark's victim, the crew found Lieutenant H. R. Kabat, *Duncan's* engineer officer. He was clinging to two empty 5-inch ammunition tanks for support. He had earlier shed most of his clothing and was bleeding profusely. His painful wounds seemed to be more slashes than direct bites, and Cooper thought his escape might be attributed to the fact that the fish was striking at the bright aluminum tanks rather than at him.

Cooper later recommended, in a written report, that these tanks be painted a dark, inconspicuous shade. The suggestion was quickly adopted. Although sharks were seen circling a few other survivors, no other such wounds were reported.

As the rescue progressed, it became systematized. Survivors who were unhurt got a quick bath (easy because they were not covered with fuel oil), some nondescript clothing, nourishment, and a bunk. The clothing and bunks were donated by the ship's company.

Alert and apparently tireless, *McCalla's* crew amazed the men they had rescued by their cheerful, single-minded disregard for their own fatigue and the prospect of its prolonged extension.

The number of casualties from wounds and burns soon swamped *McCalla's* medical officer, Lieutenant (jg) L. V. Potter, and Cooper radioed Guadalcanal for medical assistance. Another boat was sent out and met the ship at noon with three more doctors. Unfortunately, Lieutenant (jg) Fowler, *Duncan's* torpedo officer, had been too seriously injured to be helped. He died shortly after having been rescued.

All together, *McCalla* picked up nine officers and 186 men, including Captain Taylor and Lieutenant Commander Bryan. Bryan, with a young seaman, had swum all the way to Savo Island with one finger bleeding where the end had been cut off by a piece of shrapnel. He had kept the stub in his mouth after daylight to avoid attracting sharks. He and his companion had not been long on the beach when one of the landing craft came close enough to see and take them off. Four of *Duncan*'s officers and eighty-three men were not recovered. Most of them never left the ship.

The Japanese Support Group had started its rescue operations earlier than the Americans. At 4:00 A.M. *Hatsuyuki* was already overloaded with thirty-three officers and 480 men she had rescued from *Furutaka* (more than twice her own complement). Now she turned northwest, headed up the Slot, and crowded on every turn the engines could make. She left two boats at the scene, the only remaining aid she could possibly give men who might have been overlooked and were still in the water.

Sunrise, usually a cheerful time, brought only anxiety. When the American dive bombers came at 6:30, they were expected. But a plucky rescue was rewarded. All the bombs missed.

Shirayuki and *Murakumo* took even bigger chances. When they gave up their search at sunrise, they were only five miles north of the Russell Islands and sixty from Henderson Field. They were retiring at top speed on a course a little south of west. This would lead them into the Southern Track at a point about sixty miles astern of the Reinforcement Group. Again the appearance of American dive bombers was no surprise. The two ships were ready. Whatever damage the planes may have inflicted, their speed was reduced only temporarily.

The Reinforcement Group minus *Shirayuki* and *Murakumo* had continued along the Southern Track as originally planned, passing south of the Russells. At sunrise New Georgia lay on the starboard bow. At seven o'clock a B-17 was sighted, underlining the failure of the expected Japanese air cover to appear.

The big plane was apparently on reconnaissance because it did not attack. At 7:50, south of Rendova Island, three enemy dive bombers approached. There was still no air cover. Nevertheless, the dive bombers, too, tarried only briefly and departed without striking. Still unmolested, the formation crossed to the relative safety west of the two-hundred-mile mark at 9:15. Their air cover never had shown up.

At Henderson Field it was noted that the six ships sighted south of Rendova at 7:50 had only thirty miles to go to escape. It was possible, however, that the one ship seen trailing oil and possibly damaged could have been forced to stop. If all escaped, the two destroyers attacked earlier by Lieutenant Colonel Cooley should still be found.

A little after eight, therefore, another patchwork strike took off. It consisted of seven SBDs of Navy Squadron VS-3 under Lieutenant Commander Louis J. Kirn, six torpedo planes of Navy Squadron VT-8 under Lieutenant H. H. Larson, and fourteen fighters drawn from Marine Squadrons VMF-121 and 224 under Major J. Dobbin.

Again the Navy flight elements were visitors at Henderson Field thanks this time to a submarine torpedo which hit the carrier *Saratoga* on the last day of August. The fliers had been in combat at the Battle of the Eastern Solomons earlier that month.

The new strike flew a few degrees north of west, cleared the west coast of Guadalcanal, passed south of the Russells, and reached a point south of the near end of New Georgia without sighting anything. Continuing their search, the U.S. planes finally discovered two Japanese destroyers in almost the same location the two cruisers and four destroyers had been seen at 7:50, a little south of Rendova Island.

These two were steaming westward at high speed and showed no sign of damage. Since there were no protecting aircraft present, bombers, torpedo planes, and fighters separated to take position for a coordinated attack. The time was near ten o'clock.

At ten o'clock *Aoba* reached the Shortland anchorage. She had suffered many hits and would spend several months in a shipyard for repairs. Heading the list of her dead was Admiral Aritimo Goto.

By ten o'clock *Shirayuki* and *Murakumo* had advanced to a position south of Rendova Island. The dive bombing attack which had come early that morning just north of the Russells had slowed them only temporarily. In one more hour they would reach comparative safety. In the meantime, however, there was no air cover and nerves were taut.

Then the enemy planes were sighted. They struck almost at once. Fighters attacked at shallow angles, sweeping the decks with streams of bullets from masthead altitude. At the same time a fleeting glint of reflected sunlight almost directly overhead revealed a dive bomber nosing over. It was so high that it was little more than a speck in the sky. Quickly it grew. It dove so rapidly that some of the gunners, still shooting at the strafers, never saw it. When it seemed that it must crash on deck, it pulled out. A whistling shriek sounded above the bedlam of gunfire, ending suddenly as a huge geyser sprang from the water. There was no time to look. A long string of bombers was coming down on the tail of the leader.

Murakumo, zigzagging violently to spoil the bombers' aim, was drenched three times in the spray of near misses. Her lookouts may not have seen the torpedo planes skimming in close to the surface. In any case, avoiding action was not taken in time. The ship was struck by a torpedo. It disabled her engines and left her dead in the water, so badly damaged that her men knew at once she would never reach Shortland without help.

As they headed back toward Henderson, the American pilots saw that one ship had stopped. The other, apparently unhurt, had turned toward her. The planes landed safely an hour later. The hit which had disabled the enemy destroyer was credited to one of the torpedo planes.*

By this same time—eleven o'clock—Myhre and his boarding party had done all they could to save *Duncan* with their limited numbers and equipment. All holes that could be reached had been plugged. All closures not isolated by fire or flooding had been inspected and made tight.

The frequent check of draft marks at bow and stern indicated that the ship had settled only a little more since daylight. The fires forward had died down but the gutted spaces were still too hot and smoky to enter.

Weary, dirty, and hungry, the men assembled aft. Someone re-

---

* The Japanese report states that *Murakumo* was hit by a bomb. No reference of any kind is made to torpedo planes.

membered that the ship's store was outside the damaged area. A storekeeper had dutifully locked it the previous evening. Now it was broken open and a supply of candy bars taken. Eating their first meal since last night's supper, the men sat down to rest. The possibility of saving the ship seemed good, but they would have to await *McCalla*'s return for the next step. Weems, who had found paper and pencil, was making a rough sketch of the hull showing the location of the shell holes.

Their rest was suddenly ended by a sharp, clear report from somewhere forward; it was a popping sound, followed immediately by a long rumble. They quickly discovered that the forward fire room was flooding rapidly. They could not see the cause but the forward bulkhead might have collapsed at the bottom seam under the weight of water in the compartments on the other side.

They started the handybilly again, pushed the suction hose down the hatch into the rising water, and began pumping. The effort was futile. The water was rushing in much faster than the pump could draw it out. For a few minutes the space continued to fill, the pump falling hopelessly behind. Then the pump stopped. The fuel was exhausted and there was no more gasoline to be had. *McCalla*'s boat was no help. It used diesel fuel.

A moment later, when the ship lurched suddenly to port, they were abruptly reminded that the fuel failure made little difference. The bow pointed down deeper and the forward engine room started to take water. The party retreated aft. The ship settled rapidly and the water soon reached the main deck level on the port side forward. Myhre gave the order to abandon ship. At noon the party dropped into the boat from the fantail and stood off to a safe distance.

During this busy forenoon aboard *McCalla,* the able-bodied survivors had deserted their bunks. Cleaned up, dry, with something to eat and a chance to stretch out briefly, they found they were not at all sleepy. There was too much excitement to permit sleep. There was always the possibility of air or submarine attack. More important, *McCalla* continued to haul *Duncan* men out of the water all through the morning. The earlier arrivals wanted to know who had been saved and what had happened. Taylor and his officers talked with them and put together a broken thread of narrative.

The hit that had knocked over *Duncan*'s forward stack had killed most of the forward repair party. Except for two wounded who had been picked up, the entire party was missing. The seven men who had remained in the forward fire room until "everything is straightened out" were still there, consumed in the fire which had followed the explosion of one or more shells in that space.

At the same time the forward engine room, immediately aft, filled with smoke billowing through the ventilation intake. A man who was sent up to investigate found that the flames from the forward fire room threatened to sweep aft on the main deck level. They could pass through a demolished bulkhead and block all escape from the engine room, so that space was abandoned. The men arrived topside to find a frightening fire boiling up amidships, igniting everything remotely combustible in its path, and completely blocking all passage forward.

The after repair party had run out hose and was pouring water into the flames with no effect. Wounded and burned men were staggering aft. Lieutenant (jg) M. C. Broccolo, the medical officer, and B. W. Flowers, first class pharmacist's mate, were working on the growing ranks of wounded at an improvised station. (Flowers, rescued uninjured, was still assisting with the wounded in *McCalla*.) Broccolo stopped his ministrations momentarily to go forward to sick bay for more supplies. He was never seen again.

Through all of this, the after fire room and the after engine room remained undamaged. No change-of-speed commands were received after the series of hits. Telephone communications with the bridge were out and it was impossible to know what speed was wanted or even if the bridge was still manned.

Whatever the situation forward, it soon became apparent that command of the ship could be exercised only aft, and this fell upon Lieutenant H. R. Kabat, engineer officer and senior officer there.

Kabat was unfamiliar with the tactical situation and the ship's position. He had been in an engine room since sunset. Now, thrust into a new situation, he had to deal first with the most pressing emergency. Since fire was the greatest danger, he concentrated on fire fighting and turned navigation over to Ensign Frank Andrews.

Andrews, who had been at one of the after 5-inch guns during the shooting, took station at after conn. He established communications with the after engine room and the steering engine room, and brought the ship to a heading in the direction of Savo Island where she could be beached if necessary.

Though fire continued, its advance into the after part of the ship was slowly checked—so much so, that it was decided not to beach her yet. Then, with hope growing that the ship's company could outlast the fire, the remaining boilers gave out for lack of feed water.

A high-pressure marine boiler will tolerate less salt than the human body. Its supply of "feed"—the water it transforms into steam—recirculates in a closed system, leaving the boiler and flowing to the engines as steam, returning again to the boiler in the liquid state. Losses continually occur through many minute leaks in the system. These water losses have to be made up from a reserve supplied by an evaporator which makes fresh water from sea water.

Damage, however, prevented *Duncan* from replenishing the feed water for the after boilers. Any attempt to operate a boiler with insufficient water was a sure way to disable it immediately. Thus Chief Water Tender A. H. Holt, in charge in the after fire room, was forced to secure his two boilers when the water started dropping in the gauge glasses.

With steam no longer available to run the pumps which delivered salt water to the fire main, the fight was nearly over. Men below secured their machinery and came up to help the fire fighters, but there was little left with which to fight. The gasoline handybilly was brought up, but the single, thin stream of water it provided was hopelessly inadequate.

Choking smoke, hot sparks, and roasting heat waves blew down upon the men, pressing them steadily aft. Exploding ammunition added to the hazards.

Finally Lieutenant (jg) W. H. Coley and Holt led one last valiant rally. Braving scorching temperatures to return to the after fire room, they and others connected the hose from the handybilly to one of the boilers in hopes of providing water to make enough steam to operate one of the fire pumps.

Salt water from the ocean would certainly ruin the boiler but it might be a source of steam for the time needed to save the ship. The boiler was successfully lighted off. Before enough pressure could be raised, however, the steam backed up the discharge from the handy-billy and blocked it, defeating the effort. The men barely reached the topside again.

Further attempts to remain aboard in face of the flames which were consuming the ship seemed hopeless. At about two in the morning those aft took to the water. Many of the men in stations forward of the fire had already gone, most before the ship had stopped. This accounts for the widespread area over which the survivors were found by *McCalla* after sunrise.

Chapter Ten

THE END OF THE BATTLE

MYHRE AND THE OTHERS SAT IN THE BOAT for twenty minutes waiting for *Duncan* to sink, but she seemed to have stopped settling almost as soon as they had left. Heavily laden, down at the bow, and listing to port with the water lapping the main deck forward, her chances of survival seemed slim.

McCalla was out of sight. Cooper had directed Myhre to go to Tulagi if he had to abandon *Duncan* before *McCalla*'s return. But Myhre could not leave while *Duncan* still floated. At last, he decided to return for another inspection.

Once more the boat was brought up under the propeller guard and made fast and the men climbed aboard. It did not take long to discover that the ship was still settling, or perhaps she had started again.

Convinced that she was now beyond salvage, Myhre decided to speed up the sinking. He had the depth charges adjusted once more. Two or three were set to go off at thirty feet, a few at three hundred, and the rest at depths in between. While this was being done, the settling continued. Without further delay all hands jumped into the boat, the engine was started, and the line cast off.

"Back 'er down," the coxswain ordered. The engineer shifted gears and opened the throttle. The engine kicked hard, started to turn, gasped, and stalled. The engineer pushed the starter button again, shifted gears, and opened the throttle. Again the engine stalled.

Everybody watched anxiously as he tried a third time. Still the propeller shaft would turn neither astern nor ahead. The boat was still lying close to the propeller guard. The water was calm. There was no natural force that would move the boat clear in the next few minutes and there were no oars.

Everybody knew what happens when a depth charge goes off. A shock wave strikes the hull of the ship which drops it even when it is moving fast. If the charge is on shallow setting and the ship is moving slowly, the shock comes like a massive hammer blow, giving the impression below decks that the ship has struck a mine. Topside one sees a huge, spreading bush of solid water and spray stand forty or fifty feet above the surface.

The engine was behaving as though the propeller was locked. Hastily Myhre and two others tore off shoes and trousers and jumped overboard. Ducking under the stern of the boat, they quickly saw the cause of the trouble.

Remnants of bedding, life jackets, and other material which had been used to plug up holes in the ship had floated clear of the deck forward as the ship settled and had drifted aft, partly submerged. A large scrap had caught in the boat's propeller blades and had jammed between them and the fittings.

Taking turns, the three men submerged and picked frantically at the imbedded debris with knives and their fingers until their lungs ached. The stuff held stubbornly at first, resisting a knife point as though made of stone.

While the work below the surface continued, those still in the boat watched the draft marks at *Duncan*'s stern. They could tell by the slow, downward movement of the water level on the marks that the stern was rising, the bow pointing down. The end was drawing close.

Each of the men in the water made several dives. Then one surfaced with a breathless, triumphant cry. The jam was beginning to loosen. In agony those in the boat watched the stern continue to rise.

"All clear!" The three swimmers were pulled up and rolled into the boat. The propeller was backing full speed as the last man tumbled in, flopping like a fish. The engine was reversed hastily, the tiller put over, and the boat headed directly away at full speed.

Half a mile off they slowed. *Duncan* had nosed sharply downward, assuming an almost vertical attitude. Then she rotated 180 degrees on her nose, a motion which in normal attitude would have amounted to rolling over. She dove slowly until only the fantail remained above water. For three or four minutes she hung there, then started slowly to sink again.

As she disappeared, two or three of the depth charges exploded, sending up high plumes of water. What happened next was unexpected. When the spray cleared, the stern could again be seen, six feet above water. For five more minutes the ship hung stubbornly. Then, as if exhausted, she gave up and sank slowly out of sight.

They continued at half speed in the direction of Tulagi, looking back frequently. No more depth charges had exploded. Myhre wanted to know for sure that the ship had sunk finally and completely. For fifteen minutes he hung back, his concern growing. It was already after one o'clock, and there was twenty-five miles to go. Tulagi could be a dangerous place to arrive unannounced after dark. Another problem was the limited supply of fuel in the boat.

All doubts were swept away suddenly. Without warning the men in the boat felt a sharp, jarring blow as though it had run hard aground. It seemed to have been lifted from the water and dropped. A mile astern, a tremendous plume hung in the air.

Apparently the first charge to fire this time had detonated all the others at once. *Duncan* had been buried with fitting ceremony, her gravesite marked fleetingly by a tall, dissolving column of spray. She still lies in five hundred fathoms six miles north of Savo Island, squarely in the northern approach to Ironbottom Sound.

The little whaleboat headed at full speed for Tulagi. This was none too fast, and soon a much faster landing craft was sighted bearing down upon her. It was friendly, and in short order the whaleboat was in tow, its occupants passengers in the larger craft. The boarding party's luck continued, for *McCalla* was sighted in a few more minutes and the men rejoined her without further incident. After hearing Myhre's story, Cooper decided to start for Espiritu Santo, passing once more north of Savo Island and through the battle area for a final search enroute.

At 2:30, when *McCalla* reached the battle area, men were again sighted in the water. Like the members of *Duncan*'s crew found earlier, they were in small groups but not so widely dispersed. Cooper immediately slowed, and headed for the nearest.

Tired rescue details were called out again. Men stood at the forecastle rails with heaving lines. Cargo nets were dropped over the sides to provide an easy means of climbing aboard. There was excitement when the survivors were recognized. There was astonishment when the first who were approached turned and swam away from the lines which were tossed them. They were Japanese!

Cooper kicked the ship ahead a little, stopped again with the bow close to another small group. Again lines were thrown and again they were shunned. When a third offer of help was repulsed, Cooper lowered a boat with an armed detail which forcibly rescued three struggling Japanese sailors at gun point.

Some one hundred remained in the water. *McCalla* was built for a complement of about three hundred, and she already had an additional 195 survivors from *Duncan*. There was no place in the ship to lock up one hundred Japanese. Considering the frame of mind they were exhibiting it would have been suicidal to let them wander freely about the ship. Cooper recovered his boat and informed Guadalcanal he was leaving the remainder where they were.

At the same time, a third strike was taking off from Henderson Field. The command there had weighed the reports of the pilots who had attacked the two Japanese destroyers south of Rendova during the morning. Perhaps it also had received a Coast Watcher's report. There had been no air raid to disorganize operations at the field. Lieutenant Commander Eldridge was departing on his second mission of the day with six other Navy and four Marine dive bombers. He was going to the spot where the enemy ship had been torpedoed to attack any ships there now.

Arriving an hour later, Eldridge found not two but four destroyers—again without air cover. One was dead in the water; the other three were circling the cripple at high speed.

The SBDs dived out of the sun one after another from an altitude of ninety-four hundred feet. They streaked through the fire thrown up by the three circling ships. Eldridge and two of the pilots following him down were confident they had struck close. Eldridge's bomb appeared to have hit. An explosion was seen and a ship slowed and dropped out of the circle, her guns silenced. The ship at the center was also hit once, but the other two escaped damage.

The planes started back to base. When last seen, Eldridge's target was dead in the water and the ship which had been at the center of the circle was exploding. Eldridge thought it possible that the latter was already being abandoned when he had arrived and that she was now being destroyed deliberately by her sister ships.

Murakumo's situation had been reported after the 10 A.M. air attack. In response, *Nisshin* sent *Asagumo* and *Natsugumo* to assist. Whether it was decided to scuttle *Murakumo* or take her in tow is unimportant. Whatever was in progress at 4 P.M. was interrupted by the approach of Eldridge's planes. This was the third air attack of the day for *Shirayuki* and *Murakumo*.

Three ships formed a circle around the disabled fourth. The three chased each other at high speed, putting up a barrage of fire through which the attackers would have to plunge. But the barrage was not dense enough, nor the zigzagging around the circle abrupt enough. The aircraft pressed through and held their aim.

Natsugumo, part of the circling guard, took eight near misses, one or more so close that both engine rooms and other compartments were breached and flooded rapidly.* It was more load than the damaged hull could carry, and thirty minutes later she sank.

Hapless *Murakumo*, dead in the water at the center of the circle, was struck once more. There was no question now as to what her end would be.

The undamaged ships took the survivors from the other two. Then *Shirayuki* finished off *Murakumo* with a torpedo and with *Asagumo* finally reached the Shortland anchorage. They had been preceded there by the remainder of the Reinforcement and Support groups. *Natsugumo*'s captain and sixteen of his crew plus twenty-two of *Murakumo*'s company were left in the vast burial ground which had swallowed their ships.

After *McCalla*'s departure and the return of Eldridge and his pilots, only one phase of the Battle of Cape Esperance remained. But neither Scott, nor any of his captains, nor anyone at Henderson Field, nor the enemy was aware of it.

One small fraction of Task Group 64.2 was still in action very close to Cape Esperance, struggling against two opponents—the ele-

* The Japanese account does not include a direct hit.

ments and the Japanese. The American "unit" was a single rubber raft with a pair of oars and a crew of two.

While Eldridge was landing at Henderson the raft was feebly trying to make way along the west shore of Guadalcanal in the direction of Cape Esperance. Its voyage had started sixteen hours earlier from a point about two miles south and five miles farther to seaward. Now it was four miles off that point on the shore at which the northerly trend changes to northeast for the last twelve miles to the cape at the corner of the island. The two men in the raft were spelling each other at the oars, but progress was now so slight it was unnoticeable.

Besides fatigue from so much rowing, the two men suffered the discomforts of cramped quarters and exposure. The exterior dimensions of the raft were about four by six feet, so there was not even enough space to stretch out inside. In addition, it rode so low in the water that even small waves slopped in from time to time, keeping the interior wet.

The men found it best to sit on the two thwarts facing each other with the one working the oars facing forward. Their legs filled the available space and could be moved only with advance notice.

They had started the voyage in the first dark hours of the new day with sodden clothing. Their teeth were chattering long before sunrise and a turn at the oars was a welcome opportunity to work up a little warmth. Two hours after sunrise they were suffering from the heat. One of the men had tied one handkerchief across his forehead, a second across his face just beneath his eyes, and had wrapped strips torn from his undershirt around his hands and wrists.

This was Lieutenant William Tate, pilot of the *Salt Lake City* plane that had caught fire when catapulted before the battle even started. The other man was Claude Morgan, his observer and radioman.

By this time they were talking little, and when a response was called for, it came in monosyllables, a grunt, or not at all. Neither, however, had forgotten the good fortune which had preserved them since they had found themselves in flight and on fire. Tate could not have heard Morgan calling him from the left wing in those awful moments after leaving the catapult. A rapid glance astern when Morgan crawled over his head should have been enough. The entire after half of the plane was enveloped in a blinding, whirling skirt of fire.

Tate was blinded by the blaze. He couldn't see either the horizon or the surface nor could he read his instruments. He gunned the engine two or three times hoping this might put out the flames. It didn't, so he then eased down blindly toward the water with throttle and stick back and flaps full down.

The plane hit, apparently with the right wing low, dashing Morgan savagely into the water. It stopped abruptly, neither bouncing badly nor turning over.

When Morgan surfaced, he saw the plane quite close to him. But now he was on its right side as though it had spun around when it hit. It was still burning, and when he had inflated his life jacket and swum a few strokes nearer, he could see Tate still in his seat dazed. Morgan yelled insistently, reminding Tate that he was sitting over a fuel tank.

Tate at once unbuckled his safety belt and climbed out on the near wing, though he did not remember it later. He did, however, remember inflating his life jacket and swimming out to Morgan. Both of them swam farther away, fearing the fuel tank might explode.

The plane burned only a little longer. Tate signaled in the direction of the ships with a small pocket flashlight but it was pitifully inadequate and soon gave out. Then the two men swam back to see what was left. After some difficulty they found the charred carcass floating upside down.

Morgan climbed up on the underside of the horizontal tail surface. His right arm hurt so badly he could hardly use it and there was an uncomfortable cut over his right eye. He removed the burdensome weight of his web belt with the heavy .45-caliber pistol in its holster and hung it over the tail.

Tate, now fully recovered from the shock of the crash, also removed his web belt with pistol and went to work to pull the raft out of the plane. The raft was in a compartment reached from the top of the fuselage, which meant that he had to dive underneath to get at it.

The compartment opened easily enough but it took several dives to bring out the raft together with a two-gallon canteen of water. In the process Tate ripped open one side of his pneumatic life jacket but fortunately found there was adequate support in the other.

Morgan joined him in the water and together they inflated the raft. Though the fuel tank of the plane had not burned, it had developed leaks, and the gasoline floating on the water irritated the skin of both men. Tate, who had inadvertently swallowed some, was briefly sick.

Once aboard the raft, they remained at first in the vicinity of the sinking plane. Had it continued to float, they would have stayed there to be more readily seen from the air after daylight. In an hour, however, it had sunk.

Now their best bet was to try to round Cape Esperance and make the remaining twenty-two miles down the north coast of the island to the U.S. lines. The beaches in the interval and all the territory behind were in Japanese hands. They started rowing, coming in toward the coast diagonally to make some way toward the cape at the same time.

The pain in Morgan's arm had lessened, so he was able to take his turn at the oars. His keenest pain now was in the discovery that his unopened package of cigarettes had soaked through. Tate, a non-smoker, shared that particular brand of misery with him only imperfectly.

They had not been pulling very long when they saw the battle open. For them, the fight was a series of flashes over the horizon followed later by the deep echoing of guns. The flashes were easily distinguished from the lightning which had been playing on the sky in the same direction. Quiet and total darkness returned in half an hour. Even the lightning had ceased.

At daylight the voyagers found themselves about four miles offshore. Now they changed heading to parallel the coast. Abreast of them was a coconut-palm plantation and beyond it heavy jungle growth climbing a steep ridge. The ridge followed the coast toward Cape Esperance, its profile rising and falling with the outlines of several peaks.

They chose a tree close to the shore, larger than the others and with a conspicuous white trunk, so they could gauge their advance. They struggled doggedly, alternating at the oars, but made so little progress that the mark seemed hardly to have moved by the end of the day. It was very discouraging.

They guessed that they must be in a coastal current running in the wrong direction. They saw friendly planes but none saw them. They saw a Catalina seaplane orbit near the site of their crash. At least, this suggested that Henderson Field was looking for them. If they had remained where they landed, they might have been seen. Four P-39s approached later, flying very low. Tate tied his underdrawers to an oar and waved vigorously, but the fighters made no response and passed quickly from sight beyond a point of land. By the sound, they must have been attacking something beyond.

Sometime around midmorning they spotted what appeared to be a swamped boat closer inshore. After some hard rowing they reached it and found a sort of dugout canoe, perhaps the outrigger for a larger craft. There was a hole in the bottom, which Morgan plugged with his socks. After some bailing, they climbed into the dugout and took their raft in tow.

It turned out to be a much faster way to travel but the socks did not stop the leak. With more water splashing over the gunwales, they soon found they were shipping it faster than they could bail. They had to give up, abandoning the canoe for the slower but more seaworthy raft.

A happier encounter with a floating coconut followed. One of the men pried it open carefully with his sheath knife. The milk was pleasant and so was the meat. But the meat, which they consumed last, made them thirsty again.

Besides the water in the canteen, the only other refreshment on board was a package of malted milk tablets which Tate had in his pocket. At sundown they were still twelve miles short of Cape Esperance. As darkness closed in, the oars continued mechanically to reach ahead, stroke after slow stroke.

The same nightfall saw the main body of Task Group 64.2 continuing toward Espiritu Santo. Three destroyers which had been sent out to augment the antisubmarine escort had met them and Scott sent one back to accompany *Farenholt*. The next day, the thirteenth, three hours short of the anchorage, *Boise* dropped out of formation and in a solemn service committed to the deep the bodies of sixty-seven shipmates, all who had been recovered so far from the total of three officers and 104 men lost in the battle. At 3:30 P.M. the ships dropped anchor at Espiritu Santo. *Farenholt* and her escort arrived at sunset.

At dawn on the thirteenth, Tate and Morgan discovered unhappily what they had suspected all night. They had made no progress. Stiff, cold, and wet, they had somehow preserved a store of energy which was now released with the warmth of the rising sun. Perhaps they had been just beyond the edge of a favorable current and had at last entered it. Whatever the reason, they managed to round the point they had been trying to pass for twenty-four hours. The gain was a good deal more than a hard mile of water. Yesterday's tree with the conspicuous trunk was psychologically far behind. Here was new scenery. The hills seemed to rise more steeply from the water and one detected greater variety in their shapes and shades of color.

Best of all, the marks on the beach commenced to move perceptibly and it was evident that the current continued in their direction. It drew them closer to the shore, too; occasionally they were able to see the bottom.

They received visits from several sharks, big reddish-brown ones which cruised around the raft curiously, their fins cutting the water like deadly knives. Fortunately, after a few minutes' inspection the sharks departed.

During a brief shower the two men tried to catch some rain water to replenish the supply in their canteen, but without much success. There was still some water left and some more malted milk tablets. Furthermore the prospect of finding more floating coconuts seemed good.

As noon approached, the sun grew as hot as it had been the day before but now it bothered them less. They saw planes frequently and signaled several, but again without success. Nevertheless, they felt encouraged.

In the afternoon they came abreast of a long, white stretch of beach. It was covered with boats of various descriptions which obviously belonged to the enemy. They must have been used to shuttle in the reinforcements brought down by the Tokyo Express. After a closer look, they noticed that many of the boats had been damaged. Perhaps they had been the target of the strafing P-39s they had seen the day before. They observed no sign of life until suddenly the short, nasty twang of a ricocheting bullet interrupted their speculations.

In a moment they were overboard on the far side of the raft, kicking, paddling, and pulling the raft seaward. Sharks were completely forgotten. Nine or ten more shots bounced and whined fearfully close and then the rifleman gave up. Miraculously, the raft had not been hit and deflated. The two kept swimming and pulling until they were sure they were beyond range; then they climbed back in, exhausted.

It took some time to recover their strength again. Meanwhile, they watched the beach closely, but no boat put out in pursuit. They finally resumed their progress. A cautious but rising feeling of elation was crushed only a few minutes later. Off to their right they spotted what appeared to be another rubber raft, somewhat larger, colored a dull, mottled green. It bore three occupants. The odds were that they weren't friendly. When the strangers changed course and headed directly for them, they were sure they were not friendly.

Now the pistols which they had left behind were remembered. The best weapon available to them was the knife with which they had opened the coconut. They turned away and paddled frantically seaward, both working the oars. Perhaps anxiety lent extra strength, or the other raft was heavily laden. At any rate, there was no need for the pistols. Their pursuers never came close and soon gave up the chase.

When it was safe to stop, the two dropped their heads in their hands, gasping. For a long while they sat, making no effort to talk, their only movement heavy breathing. The inertia finally ended when they looked up to discover the source of a high, distant throbbing. Some small, faint gleams finally materialized into a formation of Japanese bombers so high they seemed hardly to be moving.

The same bombers were soon seen from two U.S. transports near Lunga anchorage. The ships had arrived on schedule that morning from Noumea with Army troops aboard. The transports, warned of danger, had hurriedly discontinued unloading and were under way with several destroyers around them to provide antiaircraft protection. When the bombers arrived, however, they concentrated on Henderson Field.

Two of the escorts that had accompanied the transports from Noumea, *Hovey* and *Trever,* destroyers that dated back to World War One, had been gone since morning on a separate mission. Working with aircraft, they were completing an eight-hour search of the waters west of Savo Island. They found no wreckage, no Americans. But they did find the Japanese who had been reported the day before by *McCalla*. With an additional day in the water, their aversion to capture had softened considerably and so 106 survivors of *Fubuki* were rescued, including six officers.

Nightfall found the two aviators rounding Cape Esperance. By now it seemed that they had lived their entire lives in a rubber raft. Memories of all that had gone before were like recollections from a previous existence. They had covered hardly half the distance to safety. They had drawn heavily on their reserves of energy. But the oars continued to stroke mechanically, doggedly.

After dark the wind died down completely. There was absolute silence except for the monotonous splash of the oars. They finally stopped. It seemed a good time to rest for the effort still ahead. For perhaps an hour they floated motionless and then the breeze stirred again. It came from the southeast, the direction of their distant goal. Much of a rubber raft floats out of water, relatively little is submerged to resist being pushed by the wind, so it was necessary to commence rowing again to avoid being set back precious miles. Once more one rowed while the other hunted endlessly for a comfortable position in which to lie and tried to forget that his clothes were wet and his limbs cold.

At some time during the night Morgan, who was rowing, saw a light on the beach and called Tate. The moon was down and the sky overcast and it had become pitch dark. After watching for a few minutes, the two decided the light was a large bonfire.

While one was still looking at it, the other happened to glance in the opposite direction and froze in the middle of a remark. The other turned to see a large shadow. Rapidly it grew larger and more distinct and became the towering bow of a ship advancing directly upon them, threatening to crush them. So deep was the night that they could see no more than the monstrous bow. It was a detached, spectral thing rather than the forward part of a ship. The primitive terror of a nightmare seized them as the apparition continued to expand. At the last moment it was suddenly passing, passing so close they could hear the low hum of blowers, the faint sound of a voice, and then they were flipped sharply from side to side as the bow wave swept under the raft. It was a destroyer, a two-stacker, very sleek, with splinter shields around her guns and definitely not American. She disappeared at once into the darkness.

The fire on the beach continued to burn. Now thoroughly alert, Tate and Morgan hesitated even to row. They watched and listened for other ships coming suddenly out of the night. It was possible that they were in the path of a landing operation. They tried to hear the sound of motors, voices, anything, but heard nothing. Still the fire burned. The vigil lasted a long time.

Then, far ahead in the direction they had been moving so slowly, a continuing series of flashes, like unending lightning, disturbed the darkness. A hollow, unbroken rumble, like the sounds of a bowling alley, followed. To the right of the flashes and over the island a steady glow appeared and grew. They watched with concern and experienced also a certain wry feeling of security. Henderson Field was being heavily bombarded. The shelling continued until it seemed that little could be left at Henderson to burn. Then suddenly the flashes and the thunder ceased and only the glow over the island remained. The bonfire on the beach went out as though by prearrangement.

Whatever its purpose, it had been a useful beacon. It showed that the raft was moving even without aid of the oars. Apparently a kindly current was strong enough to carry them in the right direction in spite of a contrary breeze.

After daylight the same morning, the fourteenth, *McCalla* arrived at Espiritu Santo and moored alongside *Helena* to transfer *Duncan*'s men pending their removal to quarters ashore.

When a destroyer went alongside a cruiser in a tropical anchorage during World War Two, sightseeing destroyermen often visited the cruiser to see how the rest of the world lived and to get ice cream if that was possible. Visits to the destroyer were less frequent. Lieutenant Commander Myhre, looking about his ship after the *Duncan* men left, had reason to be puzzled. He saw an excessively large number of strange faces. At first he thought some *Duncan* men had not left yet. A few inquiries confirmed, however, that the new faces were visitors from *Helena*. This was rather unusual but he continued his rounds.

He had overlooked one of the peculiarities of naval warfare, and thus was not prepared for what he saw when he entered one of the berthing compartments. The three-tiered bunks were folded back. A number of *Helena* men were there, chattering expectantly as they stood in a crooked line which bent around the end of a row of bunks and out of sight. It was like a line-up of youngsters at the ticket window of a circus. Mystified, Myhre stepped up to see what was going on.

At the end of the compartment was a space called the sail locker. Intended for the stowage of awnings, hatch covers, and other canvas, it now contained very little since most such material had been put ashore as an unnecessary fire hazard. It was separated from the berthing space by a light sheet-metal partition with a door of coarse wire mesh. It was the most suitable place on board for the detention of the three Japanese prisoners, and there they had been placed in the custody of a petty officer. They were still there, waiting transfer ashore.

Now Myhre saw the reason for all the visitors. The head of the line was at the sail-locker door. There, too, stood the petty officer. A man handed him a quarter and peered in through the wire mesh. For the quarter, the petty officer permitted him about fifteen seconds to look, then waved him on to make way for the next man. It was an entrepreneur's dream. Few commodities were as scarce in the Navy as the sight of one's enemy. What he actually looked like was a subject which could generate the most intense curiosity, particularly among those from the less cosmopolitan sections of the country. With mixed feelings Myhre halted the ingenious project and sent the *Helena* men home.

Later the same day Admiral Scott held a conference with all his captains. After hearing their comments, he doubted that his first estimate of damage inflicted upon the enemy had been complete. Everyone realized that there could be duplication, but after a long discussion and the rejection of some marginal possibilities, he revised the figures to three cruisers and four destroyers sunk, plus another cruiser and destroyer possibly sunk. He estimated the total enemy strength to have been four cruisers and six destroyers, though he did not attempt to account for the manner in which they had all reached the scene.

Captain McMorris tried to find out whether the destroyer that *San Francisco* had so nearly rammed during the battle could have been American. He learned that no U.S. destroyer had been involved in the sequence of events he described. Furthermore, no other captain was aware that any ship had passed aft on the port side in the manner seen from the bridge of *San Francisco*. In fact, they had seen no ship at all on that side except *Boise* after she had caught fire.

While this conference was taking place, Tate and Morgan were still rowing. Had they known that letters of condolence to their next of kin had already been drafted aboard *Salt Lake City,* they could not have moved faster.

The sun was oppressive and all but a quart of their water was gone. Tate's hands were bleeding but he insisted on taking his turn at the oars. The wind was still against them and they had no assurance that the current, so far more than strong enough to offset the wind, would continue. They pulled as hard as they could. The goal was in sight and they didn't relish another night afloat.

At mid-morning they had paused to watch another flight of bombers attack the hard-pressed airfield. The enemy planes were so high that although they saw two come spinning down, they never saw the fighters that had attacked them. From what they had seen it was surprising that any U.S. aircraft remained after last night's bombardment. The enemy planes split into two groups, dropped their bombs, and disappeared into the clouds. Certainly the raid had not helped conditions at Henderson Field, but it did help the two men in the raft. Bursts from the antiaircraft guns showed them the location of the field, and the approximate place along the shore where it would be safe to land.

Grimly they struggled on. The sea had become so choppy, and so much water was splashing into the raft, that continuous bailing was necessary. The endless bobbing from side to side was exhausting.

Sharks kept hanging around as if waiting for the raft to capsize. One paused so close that Morgan, in exasperation, struck him with an oar. It didn't appear to bother him greatly.

Late in the afternoon they were abreast of a clear strip of land. It seemed to mark the line between the opposing ground forces. By now their strength was giving out and they were afraid to land on even a friendly beach after dark. They changed course and started angling in toward the clear area, to land as near as possible to the American side and run for it while there was still light left.

They had just started the last leg of the journey when they saw a landing craft putting out from a beach that was definitely in U.S. territory. For a few minutes they continued to row and bail, hardly daring to believe their eyes. The boat continued directly toward them. Elated, they quit at last, opened the canteen and greedily finished the water.

The boat came cautiously alongside, a couple of the crew with rifles ready. They slung them over their shoulders as they recognized the men in the raft and leaned over to give them a hand.

"Get in quick! We're in range of a Jap field piece."

The two were hauled aboard, raft and all, and taken ashore among friends in the comparative safety of Henderson Field; sixty-seven hours had elapsed since they departed *Salt Lake City*. Thus ended the Battle of Cape Esperance.

It was only 2 A.M. of the same date in New York. A few hours later the morning papers were on the street. On the front page of *The New York Times* a large headline announced, "6 ENEMY SHIPS SUNK IN SOLOMONS BATTLE; LANDING IS BALKED . . . ," and beneath this was added, "Our ships sank cruiser, four destroyers, and transport at night—U.S. destroyer is lost." The news had been released in Washington about the hour of Scott's conference with his captains in Espiritu Santo. It reflected his first estimate, made immediately after the battle, with the addition of a transport. Whether this addition had originated with Scott or at higher level is uncertain, but it was small enough in view of Scott's latest opinion.

Chapter Eleven

"IF"

THE NEWS THAT AMERICAN FORCES CLAIMED to have sunk four destroyers, a cruiser, and a transport in addition to foiling a landing attempt could only have produced sarcastic comment at Japanese Eighth Fleet Headquarters at Rabaul. On the other hand, Tokyo's claim of two U.S. cruisers and a destroyer sunk was similarly received at Comsopac's headquarters at Noumea.

Each claim could only have looked to the other side like propaganda of the crudest sort. Neither could have credited the other with actually believing what he had reported. The Japanese would have been astounded had they known that Scott, in his revised estimate, had exceeded by one ship plus two possibles those that had been publicly claimed by Washington. They would have been amazed had they known that Scott had placed the size of the Japanese force at twice its actual number of ships. Nevertheless, Scott's figure was reached seriously, in full knowledge that any errors it caused in later estimates of enemy strength could have unfortunate results.

Scott had seen very little of what happened. The same holds true for his captains. All were influenced by the enthusiastic reports of subordinates who likewise saw very little.

For the previous two months the Americans had been depressed by the results of the Battle of Savo Island. They had not reached Cape Esperance without apprehension. What they thought they saw that night was the result of a state of mind as well as of optical illusion.

Night fires produce exaggerated effects. Two of the five Japanese ships, *Kinugasa* and *Hatsuyuki,* were damaged so slightly that they could have contributed little to the panorama of burning hulks seen by the Americans. *Fubuki* may have burned before she sank, but most of the fire seen in the direction of the enemy must have been aboard *Aoba, Furutaka,* and *Duncan.* Separate fires at the bow and the stern of either of the cruisers could have given the appearance of two burning ships. The disappearance of a target pip from the radar screen, occurring at the same time the target disappeared from the field of vision, seemed to confirm evidence of a sinking. Perhaps a better explanation—offered in hindsight—is that radar lost the target when it made a sharp turn, and the eye lost it at the same time because it had also started to lay a smoke screen.

The confused observer not only lost sight of targets that wild night, he also imagined he saw them going down. Only *Fubuki* could have sunk within view of the Americans. Nevertheless, two U.S. ships reported seeing a ship go down by the bow, screws and rudder high in the air; three reported seeing one ship break in two and roll over; and three reported a *Kako* Class cruiser sunk.

There is no way to tell which ship sank *Fubuki.* She may have been the destroyer that approached *San Francisco* during the pause in the shooting, steamed abreast of her at close range, and then tried to escape. *Furutaka* must have been the target of most U.S. ships at some time or other during the battle. Both *Duncan* and *Buchanan* probably directed their torpedoes at her, and one or more may have hit and caused the flooding which led to her loss.

Duncan, caught in the line of fire, may have been hit by American shells. But there is nothing to prove this beyond the impressions of those on her bridge and the various holes later seen on both her sides. At least some of these could have been made by Japanese shells. *Farenholt*'s damage was definitely caused by one of the U.S. cruisers.

It is not even possible to identify clearly the original targets of the U.S. cruisers, though each ship's action report states the position of its own target at the moment shooting started. When compared with each other, these positions form a pattern which does not jibe with the formation described in the Japanese account and seen by the SG radars of *Helena* and *Boise.*

The ship that approached *San Francisco* from ahead, crossed her bow from starboard to port, and disappeared down the port side of the column remains a complete mystery. Nothing is known to indicate that she belonged either to the Support Group or the Reinforcement Group but she was definitely not American.

Once the battle had started, radar was of little use except as a range finder for the guns. The lucid radar pictures that Moran and Hoover had enjoyed during the approach degenerated into an unintelligible scramble because the techniques of interpreting the rapidly changing indications in the SG scope were still in the development stage. The statement that a landing had been prevented was apparently made in ignorance of the observations of *San Francisco*'s plane. It seems to have originated at some point in the chain of command above Scott, more likely a faulty conclusion than a deliberate misstatement.

There is almost as little reason to believe that the Japanese claim was exaggerated by propagandists. The report of two enemy cruisers sunk summarizes the distorted observations made under fire in *Furutaka* and *Kinugasa*.

Only the destroyer in the score announced from Tokyo—the only U.S. ship that actually did go down—is unaccounted for in the Japanese battle report. It is possible that *Duncan* was seen by a Japanese submarine the next morning, and her fate ascertained in that manner. If wishful thinking caused the Americans to magnify a success, it caused the Japanese to minimize a failure.

When the result is victory, there is a tendency to overlook deficiencies. The careful reader, however, may wonder whether any group as difficult to control as was Task Group 64.2 deserved to win. Fire was opened by all ships at the beginning of the battle contrary to the commander's obvious intention. It was opened by two cruisers at a later stage contrary to the commander's order last received. One ship even left formation to attack without the commander's knowledge. In spite of the outstanding action of *Helena* in opening fire and of *Duncan* in attacking singlehanded, the impression lingers that discipline was poor.

In a battle between foot soldiers the men on each side maintain a certain formation, however loose, move in coordination, and fire as ordered to get the maximum effect from their weapons. But if the two sides draw close enough, the battle becomes a hand-to-hand contest. Then the confusion and intensity of the engagement preclude coordinated action. Each individual, no longer able to communicate with his fellows, becomes entirely occupied in defending himself.

This same loss of coordination can occur among ships when they stumble into hand-to-hand proximity before discovering each other. No matter how well disciplined a group of ships may be, the power to coordinate and control them will evaporate if the enemy is engaged too closely. In the meeting at Cape Esperance, command of the Support Group was completely dissolved under the force of the close American assault. Admiral Goto would have been powerless even if he had remained unhurt.

The same proximity of enemy ships and the inability to keep them continuously located and identified taxed the power to coordinate and control Task Group 64.2. *San Francisco*'s maneuver which ended with Tobin's destroyers out of formation was of secondary importance. With the enemy at point-blank range, individual captains were reacting unavoidably to immediate threats.

Admiral Scott's mistake—easily committed at night—was not lack of control but getting into a position where control was almost impossible. It is unfortunate that, since he had SG radar—the one sure means of avoiding this pitfall—he was not better acquainted with it.

With the greater difficulty of exercising command because of the closeness of the two sides came a corresponding increase in the importance of the decisions of individual captains. It was the captain of *Aoba* who, after the initial hits, made the decision to turn his ship right. In *Furutaka* the first impulse was to turn left but it was canceled by a decision to stick with the flagship.

Kinugasa, however, was not under fire, and chose not to follow the other cruisers even though it meant deserting the formation. Coming left, she dropped rapidly astern of the U.S. column and out of the battle instead of keeping abreast to be pounded to pieces before she could answer. When she was ready to shoot, she re-entered the engagement.

Hatsuyuki likewise turned left. This suggests that had *Aoba* turned left instead of right, the other two cruisers would have followed. In that case the action might soon have broken off with the Japanese cruisers still in formation, their punishment cut short. Because of Scott's doubts they might have escaped a further encounter. They might even have pulled themselves together and invited an engagement with results far less satisfactory for the Americans. The choice of *Aoba*'s captain was unfortunate but hard to criticize in the desperate circumstances which attended it.

The effect of *San Francisco*'s error in the countermarch would have been different if Captain Moran in *Boise* had treated it as an error and continued in the track of the three destroyers at the head of the U.S. column. In that case the flagship, instead of the three destroyers, would have been separated from the formation. The possibilities which could have followed are so various that speculation seems idle, but at least one is a result much less favorable to the Americans. Whatever Moran's reasoning, his choice seems the better course in light of the results.

Tobin was also forced to make a decision with serious consequences. He chose to lead his destroyers up the right rather than the left side of the U.S. column to regain station ahead. His reason was sound on the basis of all he knew. Like Scott, he knew nothing of a second section of the Tokyo Express, and supposed that opposition would be more likely to develop to the left. But had he, certainly with less justification, taken the port side, Scott's doubts would have been resolved much sooner and Japanese losses, in all probability, would have been much greater.

The most important decision made by any of Scott's captains was the one made by Captain Hoover in triggering the battle. It was the most fateful decision made on either side. If the enemy had been permitted to continue for three more minutes and if he then had opened the battle himself while crossing the T astern, he could have inflicted losses upon the Americans comparable to those of the Battle of Savo Island. Obedience, endlessly cultivated, is properly a military virtue. On rare occasions, however, an act that appears to be disobedience may be even more exemplary.

Hoover's action, coming when it did, tended to obscure the importance of another act. If *Helena* had not opened the battle, *Duncan* probably would have. How much later this would have happened, and with what result, is anybody's guess. The fact remains that Captain Taylor in *Duncan* had made a decision, a bold decision which, in the absence of Hoover's, could have been equally fateful.

All battles are subject to varying degrees of chance. But Cape Esperance was a three-sided battle with Chance the major winner. It contained an amazing number of "ifs," things that did not happen because of lack of information, accidents of timing, and miscalculation.

The darkness in which it was fought had commenced long before sundown that Sunday evening. Goto had no suspicion that a U.S. force was anywhere in the vicinity of Guadalcanal. Scott never knew that the Japanese were sending two groups of ships down the Slot that day. The B-17 that made the sighting at 10:30 A.M. and the planes that made the later sightings were all reporting *Nisshin* and her group. The Support Group, following at a distance behind, was not included in Scott's plans, which were further confused by the failure to identify *Nisshin* and *Chitose* correctly.

Twice the effects of unpremeditated timing were important. The first instance occurred when *Salt Lake City*'s plane burned. *Nisshin* and the Reinforcement Group had already passed behind the northwest shoulder of Guadalcanal. The intervening mountains screened the glare from their view. If the fire had occurred a few minutes earlier, or if the Reinforcement Group had come a few minutes later, the Japanese would have been alerted. Then any of a large number of different things might have happened. Some of these things could have been less favorable to the Americans than what actually developed.* The second case of coincidence was the meeting of Scott and Goto. If the Support Group had arrived, say, an hour earlier, it would have brought a whole spectrum of new possibilities in its wake.

Each commander made mistakes that gave the other an advantage.

* It has been stated that the glow of the same fire was sighted by the Support Group, then over fifty miles away, and that Goto, thinking it was a signal from the beachhead or the Reinforcement Group, flashed a reply several times by searchlight.

It does not seem possible that this could have happened, however, if, as stated in the action report of Cruiser Division Six, the Support Group was blanketed in rain squalls. Even if the weather and the light's intensity enabled him to see it, it is hard to believe that Goto would have replied.

There has been no suggestion as to what kind of information an uninterrupted glow on the horizon of two or three minutes' duration might have conveyed, or what kind of answer it might have required.

What could Goto have told others by flashing a searchlight except to reveal his presence, already assumed by his friends? Besides, the Reinforcement Group, if keeping schedule, was too far away to see his searchlight and so was the beachhead.

Scott did not exploit the SG radar. As a result, he approached the enemy too closely, narrowly averted a melee, and did not sink every last enemy ship as he could have. Nor did he place sufficient emphasis in his instructions on the need for captains to keep him informed by TBS. These mistakes, jeopardizing control of his command and depriving him of the ability to take decisive action at the critical moment, resulted from a lack of appreciation of the potentials and limitations of the new equipment available for night battle.

This said, it should be added that the kind of fighting that occurred at Cape Esperance had not been anticipated in U.S. naval planning; not, at least, if one is to judge by the amount of training for such combat conducted during the previous decade. The Navy had looked toward a decision in the Pacific in a meeting between columns of battleships unfettered by the proximity of land and the uncontrollable chances of low visibility. Night brushes between the light forces accompanying them were not expected to be decisive. This point of view was not unnatural, given the U.S. advantage in battleships of five to three and the well-known tendency of all military staffs to plan for the last war instead of the next. In addition, the scarcity of funds in those years limited training of all kinds, and any training for situations which seemed less critical was even more drastically curtailed. In contrast, the Japanese Navy, which had emphasized night fighting hoping to overcome its inferiority in battleships, was much better prepared for the kind of action which took place in the Solomons.

Radar and voice radio communications would take much of the chance out of night fighting. Their advantages loomed even larger when the enemy did not have radar, but these were tools too recently acquired to have been mastered. The strengths and weaknesses of the new equipment and the best procedures for its use had still to be learned by those who used it.

It is against this background that Scott's performance at Cape Esperance must be judged. A new policy of night fighting was inaugurated at Guadalcanal under the pressure of necessity. The experience of the old Asiatic Fleet at the outset of the war, even that from the Battle of Savo Island, helped only a little. How best to fight at night, how to incorporate the new equipment in the solution, had to be learned now under the enemy's guns instead of in peacetime experimentation. It fell to Scott to conduct the first, hurried experiment. Viewed in this light, the failure of his command to sink every enemy ship looks more like a successful beginning.

Of Goto's failure to have his crews at battle stations, it need only be said that it canceled all the advantages given him by Scott's mistakes.

The immediate results of the battle, beyond the losses sustained by each side, were slight. Scott saved Henderson Field a shelling but did not prevent a landing. The situation at Henderson got worse before it grew better. The naval bombardment witnessed by aviators Tate and Morgan from their raft and the air attack the next day nearly finished the field and the whole Guadalcanal campaign.

The long-range results were more substantial. The U.S. Navy gained valuable experience in night tactics and the use of the new electronic equipment. The need for a broader acquaintance with radar was illustrated and gave impetus to the establishment of training courses at U.S. bases for all who used the new gear from admiral on down.

The effect on morale was sharp. The Navy knew now that the enemy could be defeated at night, that the dark did not necessarily provide him with a sanctuary around Guadalcanal. The confidence which had been shaken by the Battle of Savo Island was greatly restored. The gross overestimate of enemy losses was, of course helpful in this respect.

Conversely, the Japanese Navy could see that the cost of supporting troops at Guadalcanal had gone up, perhaps to unacceptable levels. No longer could the Tokyo Express make the run with the certainty of going unchallenged. The Americans had displayed an aggressive leadership and a new readiness to wade in and grapple in the dark with bold disregard for possible losses. In the long run they could absorb such losses, the Japanese could not.

It was apparent, too, that American radar was a factor that would take chance progressively out of the picture to the disadvantage of the Japanese. Writing an official record for the occupation authority after the war, the Japanese authors said of this battle, "The future looked bleak for our surface force, whose forte was night warfare."

For those who seek to draw a lesson, the foremost offered by this battle is the pervasive influence of chance and the necessity of limiting it to whatever degree possible. Despite the bewildering succession of "ifs," much of the outcome at Cape Esperance hung on the simple fact that Scott had sent his men to battle stations early, Goto had not.

Chance, impersonal and indefatigable, took her toll with complete inconsistency. Inevitably, she was present at other encounters. A month later Norman Scott was killed in another flaming night battle, again within sight of Cape Esperance and in defense of Henderson Field. Hank and some of his men were lost in the same battle and *Laffey* was sunk. Eldridge, Tate, and many others on both sides at Cape Esperance were struck down in the performance of duty before the war was over. To those who remain today, the logic by which they themselves were spared is not apparent.

Looking back upon those furious nights at Guadalcanal and the multitude of blind circumstances which filled them, each can add a very humble and personal "if."

INDEX

The **Naval Institute Press** is the book-publishing arm of the U.S. Naval Institute, a private, nonprofit society for sea service professionals and others who share an interest in naval and maritime affairs. Established in 1873 at the U.S. Naval Academy in Annapolis, Maryland, where its offices remain, today the Naval Institute has more than 100,000 members worldwide.

Members of the Naval Institute receive the influential monthly magazine *Proceedings* and discounts on fine nautical prints and on ship and aircraft photos. They also have access to the transcripts of the Institute's Oral History Program and get discounted admission to any of the Institute-sponsored seminars offered around the country.

The Naval Institute also publishes *Naval History* magazine. This colorful quarterly is filled with entertaining and thought-provoking articles, first-person reminiscences, and dramatic art and photography. Members receive a discount on *Naval History* subscriptions.

The Naval Institute's book-publishing program, begun in 1898 with basic guides to naval practices, has broadened its scope in recent years to include books of more general interest. Now the Naval Institute Press publishes more than sixty titles each year, ranging from how-to books on boating and navigation to battle histories, biographies, ship and aircraft guides, and novels. Institute members receive discounts on the Press's nearly 400 books in print.

For a free catalog describing Naval Institute Press books currently available, and for further information about subscribing to Naval History magazine or about joining the U.S. Naval Institute, please write to:

Membership & Communications Department
U.S. Naval Institute
118 Maryland Avenue
Annapolis, Maryland 21402-5035

Or call, toll-free, (800) 233-USNI.